DOWNSIZING FOR TINY LIFE

Go from a house full of stuff to a life full of adventure

CHRIS DICROCE

FOREWORD BY CAROLYN SHEARLOCK

Tin Finch
tinfinchpress.com

What They're Saying

"Chris is a true downsizing expert. He addresses the main problem with getting rid of stuff: our emotional attachment to clutter. You'll love his step-by-step process of downsizing, from identifying the junk in each room of your house, to properly listing and selling your belongings, to deciding what to keep and what to trash. You'll feel much lighter once you finish this book, whether you plan on living tiny or just a more minimalist life. As a person who's downsized to live in a campervan and a sailboat, I can vouch Chris really knows what he's talking about."

- Kristin Hanes, The Wayward Home (thewaywardhome.com)

* * *

"Downsizing For Tiny Life is an invaluable tool for anyone contemplating moving aboard. The information he shares will shift your mindset around downsizing from one of dread to one of exalted possibility. I appreciate how he organizes the information and utilizes checklists. He offers up concrete suggestions about how to tell what's junk and what isn't. I highly recommend Chris's book.

- Nica Waters, serial cruiser, instructor at Cruiser's University, and podcaster at The Boat Galley Podcast

* * *

"Chris' witty humor and writing style helps take you step by step through what is otherwise a painful process and makes it simple and effective."

- Kathryn L., Sailor

* * *

"Great job in putting together suggestions, cohesive lists, plans of actions and other ideas to help us through this time after years of antiquing/collecting and holding on to all those tchotchkes we hold near & dear! Sure did put me in a 'detached' state of mind and made 30+ years of downsizing easier than I ever thought possible. Much thanks & highly recommend!"

- Jill Wylly, Homeowner

* * *

"This is written in a fun and easy style... Downsizing ain't fun and having what feels like a friend to cheer you on and joke around with you makes it much easier!"

- Cheryl Fuhs, Sailor

Table of Contents

Foreword

"Sell everything and live on a boat." It sounds so simple. That is, until you go to do it. I should know, I've done it not once, but twice.

I swore, after the first time, that we wouldn't accumulate "stuff" when we moved back ashore. But you know what? We did.

I'm convinced that if there is space, we find stuff to fill it. And then, that very "stuff" holds us back from what we really want to do.

The problem is two-fold: the emotional attachments to items, and the overwhelming nature of the task.
You walk through your home and open a closet. How do I decide what to do with all this? And then you realize how many other closets you have. Not to mention drawers. Bookcases. Boxes in the basement and attic. There's just too much, you think. *It's an impossible job.*

If you actually do get started on the project, the next problem arises as you consider various items. For me, it was my mom's good china, which she revered as it had been **her** mother's. And the (expensive) china cabinet I'd bought to store it in. Never mind that I'd used the china exactly twice in the 20-odd years it had been mine.
The first time we "sold it all" we didn't actually sell everything. I made a deal with my husband – I'd sell the china cabinet but keep the china and put it in storage.

And when we moved back to land after 7 years of cruising, I bought *another* china cabinet to house it.

I hadn't known Chris when I did the big purge the first time. I hadn't had any sort of a plan of attack. On one hand, I kept stuff I shouldn't have and on the other, I resented my husband for convincing me to get rid of some of my treasures.

While we were living on land, I got to know Chris' wife, Melody, online through some cruising Facebook groups. A year later, when we were going to be traveling through Hollywood, Florida where they were, Melody and I made arrangements for the four of us (plus dogs!) to meet up for lunch.

Somehow, in the course of that lunch, we started talking about how we'd moved back to land with very little "stuff" and five years later, had a (small) house full. That led to talking about downsizing, the problems inherent in it, and Chris told a little of his thoughts about it. What I might call a quick summary of what you'll find in the introduction to this book.

A year and a half later, we'd bought our second boat, spent six months on it and decided we weren't going back to living on land. I was going to have to downsize again, and I was going to have to face that china again. This time, though, I had some help, in the form of that quick conversation with Chris. I remembered what he said about how to approach the project, and how to make what had previously been such hard decisions. I'm sure Chris doesn't even remember that we talked about downsizing that day at lunch, let alone that his words would have stayed with me. But they did. And they made a difference.

A big difference.

That second time, downsizing was a manageable experience. I wasn't stressed. I wasn't in tears. And yes, I got rid of my mom's china . . . by giving it to a friend who always dreamed of owning a set like it.

When we returned to town a year later and stayed with her, I was thrilled to see my former china on her table. I had downsized without resenting "giving up" my treasures or keeping things I clearly wasn't using.

In this book, Chris has created a complete system for downsizing. It's a full step-by-step how-to, starting with the necessary mindset and laying out a series of very specific tasks. Too many "how-to's" only give a top-level view of the tasks to be done, which doesn't give the reader the tools to actually complete them. Chris is one of the rare writers who gets into the nitty-gritty.

Detailed, actionable steps in bite-sized chunks and the encouragement to do each one. He lays out a complete path that will get you from a full house to your tiny home.

Carolyn Shearlock, Author of *The Boat Galley Cookbook* and founder of TheBoatGalley.com

Join the Insider List

Join Chris DiCroce's Insider's List for exclusive content and to be the first to find out about new releases, contests, and more. Visit chrisdicroce.com to subscribe.

Bonus Resources

There are several free resources that accompany this book to make your downsizing process easier. You can access the Resource Hub at chrisdicroce.com/tinylife.

Introduction

Welcome to Downsizing for Tiny Life! I'm happy you're here.

Professional Organizer Andrew Mellen once said, "When everything is precious, nothing is precious." That's one of the most powerful quotes I've ever read. When we apply this sentiment to the topic of downsizing, it becomes pretty clear as to why we as a society have so much trouble getting a handle on our addiction to stuff. If we believe that everything we own means something or holds a measure of our wealth, we'll have so much more difficulty being objective when it comes time to get rid of something.

These days, the pressure to do more and do it faster is more intense than ever before. We're under a 24-hour marketing assault telling us to "Eat this! Drive this! Wear this! Drink this! And buy, buy, BUY!"

We've accumulated more stuff, but less happiness. More gadgets, but less time for family, friends, or ourselves.

Is this you? Are you one of the 25% of Americans who can't even park a car in their 2-car garage because it's packed with other crap? If so, that's okay. There's no judgment here. Only solutions. The fact that you're here means you're ready for a change.

I know what it feels like to want a big change. Back around 2009, I was living in Nashville, working a soul-crushing job. And no matter how much I worked, budgeted, and cut expenses, I always seemed to have just enough to pay the bills, but never enough to make strides toward savings or investments. I was done. Ready for a big change. A massive change.

During that time, my only refuge was a small sailboat I kept at a local boat club. It's where my then girlfriend Melody (now wife) and I spent most of our time when we weren't working. It was the only place I felt at peace. And during those moments of peace, a seed was planted.

Fast forward to 2012. Melody and I quit our jobs, sold our house, and got rid of almost everything we owned to move aboard a 35-foot sailboat. You can read about that terrifying, yet liberating experience in my book, *You Gotta Go To Know*. In that book, I discuss the fear of quitting our jobs, selling our house, and explaining to our friends and family why we were getting off the hamster wheel. I also touch on the specific and personal emotions we felt as we downsized and how we dealt with them.

For us, downsizing was a fairly quick, but still difficult process, even though we were emotionally ready to go. Personally, by the time we listed the house, I was tired of looking at all the crap I'd accumulated. I wanted a simpler life, one filled with experiences, not stuff. Initially, Melody wasn't as gung-ho as I was, but after many long conversations, tears shed, and deep breaths, we made the leap to move onto a boat and agreed to reassess everything after one year of living aboard.

We've been gone since 2012, and we've sailed to Cuba, Mexico, Belize, and Guatemala and have seen some of the most spectacular places in the world. And if you ask me whether I miss my crockpot, lawnmower, or storage shed full of shit, I'll say, "Hell no!"

I recently asked Melody, if I gave back her fancy shoe collection and closet full of designer clothes, and in exchange, I'd take back the experiences we've had since we left our old life behind, would she trade? Without a second's hesitation, she said, "Absolutely not!"

The fact that you're reading this means that you're also ready for a change, and oh boy, are you gonna change! Let me tell you this straight up. By the end of this book, if you tackle the tasks as I lay them out for you, you're going to transform your life. I know that sounds dramatic, but I did it and my life has indeed been transformed. And if I can do it, you can do it!

If you implement what I've outlined here, by the end of the book, you'll have:
- More time for family and friends
- More money to save and invest
- More freedom to travel
- Less stress

And… you'll be able to finally realize your dream of living a simpler, more manageable life.

It's highly likely that during this process, you'll utter the phrase, "Holy shit. What have I done?" more than once.

This book is laid out in sections. Each section will focus on achieving one major goal. I've broken each major goal into 5 individual tasks. This helps to eliminate the usual 'where do I start?' overwhelm. It simplifies the process because your focus is on completing one task at a time. You know the adage; how do you eat an elephant? One bite at a time.

For this process to work, you're going to have to commit. Focus and intention are two of the biggest requirements for being successful when you want to downsize. You already have the intention. Whether it's to move onto a sailboat, into a van, RV, or tiny house, or even just downsizing to simplify your life, I've got you covered!

I want you to be successful. And if you follow the tasks as laid out in this book, I know you will be.

FREE RESOURCE HUB

First things first. To make this entire process easier, I've put together a Resource Hub where you can download or print tools, checklists, and documents I talk about in this book to make your downsizing process easier.

Visit the Resource Hub at chrisdicroce.com/tinylife.

Start Here: The Foundation

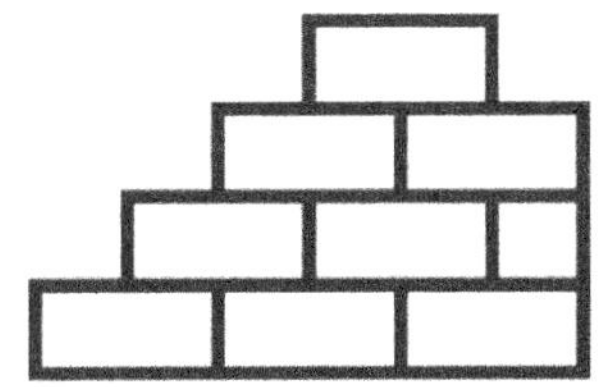

The Psychology of Stuff

Why Are We So Attached?

*"A man's Self is the sum total of
all that he can call his."*
-William James, The Principles of Psychology, 1890

Before we go into the actual process of downsizing, I think it's important to understand the psychology associated with our stuff. It might help explain why we have such a hard time getting rid of it.

In 1890, when William James wrote those words, your wealth might have been determined by the number of cattle or acreage you owned. Well, times have changed. BMW, Rolex, Gucci, and Apple have replaced the cows, and they don't smell nearly as bad!

We as a society have also changed. We've become obsessed with this stuff. We've perfected the *art of ownership*. We're addicts, and for over a century, really smart people have been trying to figure out why.

In 1932, Swiss child psychologist Jean Piaget published a study that determined our attachment to stuff begins shortly after birth. It strengthens through adolescence and into adulthood, where we link our *stuff* directly to who we are and what we've achieved in life. Cars, jewelry, and clothes accentuate our personalities. Houses become beacons of success. They're our adult trophies. They scream, "Look what I've achieved!"

As a society, we've accumulated so much stuff that the idea of going through it, sorting it, and donating, or throwing it away is so overwhelming that many never even attempt it. Do you know how most of us deal with the overwhelming clutter in our lives? We rent a storage unit (a place different from the place we already own) and we stuff it full. Then we pay good money to pretend it doesn't exist.

- Today, 25% of American homeowners can't fit a car inside their 2-car garage.
- The average American spends 55 minutes a day (that's 12 days per year), looking for things they *know* they own, but can't find.
- And 80% of what we own, we never use. Think about that!

Let's take a look at a few things, emotional explanations or trigger points, if you will, that might help explain why it's so difficult for us to let go of our belongings.

1. Endowment Effect: In 1980, Richard Thaler, a Behavioral Economist, arrived at the theory that *people place a higher value on things simply because they own them. They would demand considerably more to give up an object than they would to initially acquire it.*

How does that translate into your modern-day dilemma? Well, that pair of Rossignol ski boots you bought in 1987 for $400 is keeping you from enjoying a less stressful life – because you refuse to sell them for less than you paid!

2. The Someday Factor: In your attic sits a dusty easel and a hundred tubes of dried oil paints, also dusty. They represent a time, in the future, where you're going to "get back to painting." In your mind, those items represent everything that "could be."

We think like this all the time. And it's another factor that keeps us from getting rid of those items that *represent* something we define as special. "Someday, I'm going to fit into my high-school letterman jacket, prom dress, skinny jeans."

The truth is, there will be no someday when you are stressed out, working 80-hour weeks, and living paycheck to paycheck. Under those circumstances, *someday* will always remain on the horizon. You have to actively take the necessary steps to give yourself more time and **allow someday to be today.**

Since I downsized, simplified my life, and moved onto a sailboat, I've written and published multiple Amazon bestselling books and sailed to eight countries.

Free Time = Free Mind.

3. Maybe it's Genetic! Yes! How cool is this, a chance to pass the buck, blame somebody else for your deficiency? Ladies and gentlemen, I give you, the *Sunk Cost Fallacy* and its sidekick, *Loss Aversion*. That's a mouthful! But I'm gonna explain.

Behavioral economist Dan Ariely writes in his book, *Predictably Irrational*, "When factoring the costs of any exchange, we tend to focus more on what we may lose rather than on what we stand to gain."

The *Pain of Paying*, as he puts it, arises whenever you must give up anything you own. The amount doesn't matter at first. You'll feel the pain no matter what price you pay, and it will influence future decisions and behaviors.

Basically, this theory comes down to: *I can't get rid of those ski boots! They cost me $400.00!* You have that number stuck in your head even though you purchased them many years ago. Can I just mention that those boots are now the same age as the space shuttle!

Let 'em go, baby. Let 'em go.

To help you see the light, here's a little truth about retail markups on the common items we purchase. This will hurt your feelings.

- Jeans: 100 - 350% above wholesale! (Does a 20% off sale get you excited now?)
- Shoes: 100 - 500%
- Eyeglasses: 800 - 1,000%
- Furniture: 200 - 400%

Mr. Ariely complicates things a bit more, believing these traits associated with risk and loss can be passed down from generation to generation. I think it's time to break the chain!

Whether or not you believe the genetic connection is real isn't important. What *is* important is that you use it as another bit of information to help you understand why you may be holding onto so much stuff. Once you understand it and can see an item's true monetary value versus a perceived internalized value, you can address it.

4. The Emotional Rescue. This one is a biggie. The explanation? You just *can't* give it away. "Aunt Darla gave that to me. It's special." You've attached a connection to an object. A connection that you feel will be severed when and if you get rid of that object.

That object, Aunt Darla's porcelain gravy boat, represents a happy period during your childhood. You associate her with positive, loving memories. If you get rid of the gravy boat, you get rid of the memory.

Let me tell you, those feelings, memories, and connections don't belong to the object. They belong to you.

PRO TIP: Regift the gift! Yep, give the item back to whoever gave it to you. Now, each time they see the item, it will remind *them* of *you*. I call these **Turnabout Memories.** When and if you ever decide you need that gravy boat back, I betcha Aunt Darla will still have it and will gladly return it to you.

AUTHOR NOTE: These are just a few examples of theories that we use to keep us holding on to things and I've tried to add a bit of humor here. I want to take a moment and clarify a bit before I move on. Some of us go into the downsizing process with excitement and anticipation for what's to come in our new lives. Yes, there is some fear, but for the most part, it's a positive experience.

That being said, if you're downsizing due to a tragic event like the loss of a spouse or a divorce, I am certainly not making light of those circumstances. Having been through a divorce, I wouldn't wish it on anyone.

Even if your decision to downsize is not due to a tragic loss or life event, it's still a difficult and emotional process because downsizing itself becomes the *big life event*. It's a change and whether you're at the beginning of the change or towards the end, the chances are high that you're experiencing some type of stress. But I'm here to tell you, it's worth it. Whatever you're going through, keep going. A movement has begun. Many people are seeking a change. And just like you, they don't want *more* anymore. They want *better*.

As you go through this process, I think it's really important to understand that less doesn't mean nothing! It's so important to know this, that I'm writing it again.

LESS doesn't mean NOTHING.

You're not getting rid of everything you own. You're paring down to the most essential items and keeping the things that mean the most to you. And while you may own less, you'll most likely be able to afford better quality items. If you don't have thirteen different suits or sweaters, you can afford that one nice, custom suit or that beautiful, hand-made cashmere sweater, guilt-free. Not a bad trade-off if you ask me.

So now you have a better understanding of why we're so attached to our stuff. Keep this in mind as you go through the rest of this book because it will help on those emotional days when this process seems daunting or even impossible.

Know Your Why

What's your motivating force?

Whether you think about it this way or not, a sailboat or RV is a tiny house, and if you haven't noticed, these days... tiny is big. Blogs like Tiny House Blog and magazines like Dwell devote themselves to keeping up with the latest designs and developments. TV shows like Tiny House Nation or Tiny House, Big Living are hugely popular. And YouTube is rife with videos from people living in vans, converted school buses, and even shipping containers. Small and simple.

Why? Why have thousands of people around the globe taken such drastic action to change and simplify their lives? I think if you asked each one the same question, you'd get many different answers but buried deep within each of those answers you'd uncover an unmistakable theme, the desire for a simpler existence.

I believe it's the most important question to ask before you ever touch an item in your house.

Why?

Why do *you* want to make this change? Everyone has a different reason, and you need to know yours. It's critical really. It's the one constant that will keep you on track. Your why is the big red pin that marks the destination on your road map. Yes, the road will wind, and you'll be faced with detours here and there, but knowing your why allows you to stay focused on the destination.

- Is it a financial choice? Are you trying to free up cash or pay off debt?
- Do you want more time with family and less time in the office?
- Do you want to improve your relationship?
- Do you want more money to travel?
- Maybe you're just seeking a simpler, less-cluttered life?

Whatever it is, you must know your WHY. Write the question: **Why do I want to live tiny?**

Try to answer that question in one paragraph or less. One sentence is even better. Distill it down to the tightest phrase. Laser focus. It's going to be your battle cry.

- I want to be debt-free.
- I want the freedom to chase the sun.

- I want to make a life. Not just a living.

Keep a journal of your process and your progress. If you're like me, I love to write things down. I keep a small notebook with me all the time. Use your phone, or maybe even start a blog.

Choose what's easiest for you. Pick the format that you *know* you'll use.

Why do I suggest writing it all down? Well, it's proven that writing things down and making lists positively affects productivity. Once you write down that thought or idea, your mind is free from having to hold onto it. It's now free to think and solve other problems. It's like downsizing your mind!

For this exercise, writing down your Why serves three purposes:

- It frees your mind to let go of the thought

- It gives you a visual reminder of what the goal is
- Knowing Your Why will keep you focused and excited

Physically writing out your why means that you don't have to remember it. It's right in front of you. It will help you when you start to feel bogged down. And that *will* happen. It's natural, but don't let it derail you.

When I went through my downsizing process, I taped a photo of the sailboat I'd been dreaming of to my bathroom mirror. It was the last thing I saw at night before going to bed and the first thing in the morning to start my day. It was a subtle way to remind me of what I was working towards.

Keep a few things in mind here. You don't have to have your boat, RV, or tiny house to start downsizing. You just have to set your intentions and begin the process of changing the way you think about stuff. In fact, I highly recommend that you start this process well in advance of when you think you'll need it. It always takes longer than you think.

Now, if you already own your future tiny space, that's great. You know exactly how much room you have to work with. You also know the amount of storage and closet space that's available and that's huge.

Those of you who are renting have it a bit easier. You don't have to worry about selling a home. Others might be empty nesters who've lived in the same house for 25 years. You have decades to sort through. It will take you a little longer. What matters is that you keep your eye on the prize and keep moving towards your goal.

Remember that battle cry you wrote down? Your WHY? Well, it doesn't expire!

Now, here's a small assignment to get you taking immediate action towards your downsizing for tiny life. When this process kicks into gear, you're going to divide your belongings into different groups:

- Things to keep
- Things to sell
- Things to donate/recycle
- Things to trash

To get you started, I want you to decide where you're going to put the money you make from selling your items. Don't just stick it in the bank. Watching the money increase as you go through this process gives you positive reinforcement. It's a tangible indication that what you're doing is working. You'll see that it doesn't take long to make a thousand dollars or more!

I recommend a **fireproof document bag** for two reasons:

1. It's cheap
2. Once you're done with your downsizing, you can continue to use it to store:
   - Passports

- Boat / RV or any relevant documentation
- Medical information
- Other important banking and credit card information

In full disclosure, we started with an old mason jar with a piece of tape on it labeled BOAT FUND. Not very original I know, but it's simple.

Okay, here we go. All the fluffy intellectual stuff is out of the way. You now know the psychology behind your addiction to stuff and you know your Why. You have your secret stash for all those dollars you're about to make, and you're rubbing your palms together saying, "Let's do this!"

ACTION STEP

Decide on a fun place to put the money you make from the items you sell. Write your WHY on a Post-It note. Stick it on your bathroom mirror or refrigerator, or better yet, both!

Section 1:
All About the Junk

junk

noun /jəNGk /

*old or discarded articles that are considered
useless or of little value.
Synonyms: rubbish, clutter, odds and ends,
bric-a-brac*

Let's get busy! This section is all about the junk. The bric-a-brac.

Bric-a-brac! I love that. I'm bringing bric-a-brac back! Okay... I'll calm down. Whatever you decide to call it, we're going after all of it. The low-hanging fruit. The rotten stuff. The stuff that you know is junk, but just can't label it as such.

With each task, you're going to tackle a different room in your home. By the end of this section, you'll be blown away by the amount of pure, unadulterated crap that surrounded you. It might even be more shocking than what's under your couch right now.

> *"The journey of a thousand miles*
> *begins with one step."*
> -Lao Tzu

Here's a little tidbit before you get started. You didn't accumulate all this stuff in one day, and you're not going to be rid of it in one day either. It's going to be a journey, yes, but not of a thousand miles.

And you've already taken your first step. You're here!

ACTION STEP

Visit the Resource Hub (chrisdicroce.com/tinylife) and print the Junk Checklist. This list is by no means the last word when it comes to defining junk, but it's pretty darn close. After all, I don't know you personally, nor do I know the size of your home or your garage. I have no idea if you have 17 sets of golf clubs or every Tom Cruise DVD ever made. The Junk Checklist is a guide. Use it. Add to it. Change it. Make it work for you.

Task 1:
Lighten the Living Room!

This entire section is geared toward getting rid of the obvious junk. Not much thought or pain should be involved in this one.

Again, we're going after the low-hanging fruit here.

For this task, I highly recommend grabbing a few clear plastic bins from Amazon or your local home goods store. Grab some painter's tape and some black markers for labeling the bins.

You'll use these bins throughout this entire process. And they're great because:

- They're clear so you can see what's inside
- They're resistant to moisture and bugs
- They're easy to carry and stack

PRO TIP: I strongly advise against using cardboard for anything you'll be storing for any length of time. Cardboard is dreadful for preventing moisture, mold, and bugs. Only use it for trash or transporting.

Now that you have your bins, markers, and tape, label one bin DONATE and a second bin TRASH.

Now, go through your entire living room, using the Junk Checklist as a guide. Some of the items that are immediate grabs are:

- Old magazines and newspapers
- DVDs and out of date video games
- Burnt to the nub candles
- Busted remotes (that you have no earthly idea what they control anyway).

These items immediately get relegated to either the RECYCLE or TRASH bins.

I know you love your DVDs, but everything is digital now. There's no sense lugging them all over the place only to find out later that you have no room in your new life. Trust me, they aren't worth enough to warrant going through the trouble of listing them to sell. Donate them to a local library, school, or nursing home.

This task should take you no more than an hour. Be honest. Be ruthless. If you finish in 20 minutes, great.

Don't lose too much sleep over throwing out that Home & Garden magazine from 1997. Admit it, you were never going to use that recipe for chickpea meatloaf!

Okay, a huge congrats on completing your first task. That was no sweat, right? Give yourself a big, fat high-five. You're one step closer to your new decluttered life!

ACTION STEP

Set a timer for one hour. Grab the Junk Checklist, crank up your favorite music, and go through your living room. Be quick. Be brave. Be ruthless. You'll be surprised at how much you can clear out once you put your mind to the task and put it into action.

JUNK CHECKLIST - LIVING ROOM

❏ Burnt to the nub candles or candles you never burn
❏ Old DVDs and video games
❏ Broken or unused remotes
❏ Old dog toys
❏ Books you don't read
❏ Junk mail
❏ Newspapers
❏ Old Magazines
❏ Potpourri diffusers
❏ Board Games

❑ Fake house plants / dead house plants

❑ Art you don't like

❑ Figurines or knickknacks

❑ Damaged or worn furniture

Task 2:
The Bathroom, By God!

Question: If you're American in the living room, what
are you in the bathroom?
Answer: European

I know. I know. That joke was lame. You have no idea how difficult it is to find quality toilet humor.

And, speaking of that, I'd bet the state of your bathroom is no laughing matter right about now. That's okay. We're gonna make some strides in this task.

And remember, right now, we're only dealing with the obvious junk! Don't go too crazy unless you're inspired. Then...go crazy! Toss those blown blow dryers and crumby curling irons. How many rusty razors does a man need? I'll answer that... None!

Seriously, outside of the kitchen and the garage, I believe the bathroom may be the most difficult space to downsize. Because, if you're like most people, you've stockpiled numerous fancy-smelling shampoos, conditioners, shave gels, and razors; certain that each one is essential for your daily beautification process.

Today is the day we face that medicine cabinet and liberate those shower racks! Grab your Junk Checklist (in the Resource Hub or at the end of this task), and let's get started.

Toiletries / Makeup: This is a biggie. Along with cluttering up your bathroom, these things could be wreaking havoc on your health.

Did you know that the average woman uses 12 personal care products or cosmetics a day – containing over 168 different chemicals? Some of these chemicals are toxic to young women. What's worse, the cosmetic companies have no legal obligation to report health problems from their products to the FDA.

If you have a favorite shampoo, conditioner, or makeup brand, use it until it's gone. When you need to restock, think about replacing those nasty, chemical-laden products with some healthier options. Many companies offer natural shampoos, toothpaste, and chemical-free makeup.

On our boat, Dr. Bronner's Pure-Castile Liquid Soap was our main go-to soap. Not only is this stuff certified organic, but the packaging is also made from 100% recycled materials and you can use it as your body wash, shampoo, or in your laundry. And, it's one bottle!

Now's a good time to mention... biodegradable is BIG DEAL!

Your tiny life will present an entirely new set of challenges and perspectives. When you're bathing or shampooing in your boat, RV, or tiny house, the products you use have a greater impact on the environment around you.

If you're on a sailboat, the products you use will drain directly into the water. By choosing biodegradable cleaning and bath products, **you won't have to worry about harming the reef or the fish**! In a tiny home or RV, you'll collect them in your grey water tank. Not as big a deal. But when it's time to dump that stuff, why not dump stuff that isn't so harmful? Win-win for everyone I say.

Expired Medications: Go through your medicine cabinet and pull out all of your old prescriptions. There are many ways to dispose of old medications. You may be tempted to simply chuck expired meds in the trash.

Please don't do this! You never know if a kid or an animal/pet will find this stuff.

The FDA has a great website dedicated to the safe disposal of medications – just search for "FDA medication disposal" and you should find it. I'll briefly summarize but I suggest you check it out for the full story.

- Ask your pharmacy if they offer medicine take-back options
- Remove all labels and personal information from containers
- Don't crush or flush the tablets

The FDA states that it's okay to mix the medicine with coffee grounds or dirt first, then sealing them in plastic bags. I implore you to seek other options before adopting this method. It seems like a really bad idea. I only mention it because some folks want the path of least resistance and I see this as one step above chucking it all in the trash with no countermeasures. Safety first!

Old Towels & Washcloths: If you're like most people, you have ratty towels and washcloths lying around that for some reason, we all feel the need to hang onto. Get rid of them. If they're in decent shape, put them in the donate bin. If they're stained with mascara or full of holes, toss 'em.

Right now, you *should* have a bin full of shampoos, conditioners, and toiletries for ready donation and a bin full of makeup and other stuff to trash. The products that remain should be your absolute, can't-live-without favorites, and there should be considerably less of them.

Grab your notebook or make an entry in your journal about how this went for you. Are you excited to try new, healthier products?

If you need a virtual hug, go back and read your WHY. Go in and look around your lightened living room. Whatever you have to do to stay positive and feel that you've accomplished something, do it. That doesn't mean purchasing something new!

Stay focused on your goal. Your WHY. Don't get discouraged. We're just getting started.

ACTION STEP

Using the Junk Checklist, go through your bathroom and box up or trash old makeup, toiletries, towels, and other 'junk'. Dispose of old medications responsibly. Reward yourself with a self-care day using some of your favorite can't-live-without items.

JUNK CHECKLIST - BATHROOM

❑ Old / unused / almost empty bottles of shampoo & conditioner

❑ Old or excessive bath towels (keep no more than 2 per person)

❑ Old or excessive washcloths

❑ Old or extra hair dryers & curling irons

❑ Old disposable razors or rusty razor blades

❑ Expired or unused medications (<u>FDA proper disposal advice</u>)

❑ Old makeup or makeup you never wear

❑ Dried up nail polish or shades you never wear

❑ Bad-smelling perfumes or deodorants

❑ Sample-size anything

❑ Soap wafers

❑ Bottles of anything you haven't used in over 3 months

❑ Excessive sunscreens, hand lotions, hair products

❑ Cleaning products

Task 3:
Kitchen Aide

So far, you've lightened your living room, tackled some of the obvious overages in the bathroom, and now it's time to deal with one of the more challenging rooms in your home. The kitchen. For all you non-boaters, the "kitchen" on a boat is known as the galley.

Again, just to reiterate, in this section, we're only going after the obvious stuff.

With your Junk Checklist in hand, you have a good indication of what we're going for on this first run through the kitchen. Here are just a few of the items that you're gonna target:

- Mismatched / lidless containers
- Single-use plastic bags
- Chipped dishes or mugs
- To-go containers and take out menus
- Stained or worn hand towels and pot holders
- Excessive reusable shopping bags
- Old cookbooks and cutting boards
- Dull knives and rarely used utensils: cheese slicers, fondue / shish kabob skewers

A lot of this stuff will be perfectly fine to donate. I don't recommend trying to sell your chipped mugs or mismatched Tupperware. The effort expended won't match the monetary reward.

When we get into the serious downsizing, your valuable cookware, utensils, and place settings can definitely be turned into cash. For now, in this section, we're going with a donation strategy. The rest can be trashed.

Once you've gone through your kitchen cupboards and drawers, it's time to tackle the proverbial JUNK DRAWER that every kitchen seems to have. This drawer has an over-abundance of:

- Old batteries
- Excessive corkscrews
- Dried ink pens
- Chopsticks

- Rubber bands
- Mystery keys
- Paper clips and matchbooks
- Condiment packets

WHERE DO I TAKE THIS STUFF?

Now that you're this far into the downsizing process, you probably have several things ready to go for donation.

If you live close to a Goodwill, Salvation Army, or Veterans Donation Center, I recommend throwing that donate bin in the car and taking it to the donation center of your choice immediately! Make sure to keep the bin.

Dropping it off immediately does two things:

- It prevents you from changing your mind
- It gets that clutter out of the way

If you don't want to make a bunch of trips back and forth, stage that bin in a spare room or garage. It's the beginning of your donate stack.

Other options to consider when donating:

- Homeless shelters
- Veterans Assistance Centers
- Schools (especially for art supplies)
- Donation boxes (usually found outside your local grocery stores)
- Hospitals (*unused* makeup for cancer patients)

- Nursing homes
- You can also do a Google search for other donation options in your area

Donating to people in need gives this exercise an entirely different perspective.

This first run-through of the kitchen should take about an hour. Remember, we are just tackling the obvious JUNK in this task. Very little pain should have been caused by tossing that Benihana menu from 2011.

Now, take a moment to look around and congratulate yourself. Imagine yourself walking down the dock or taking in the view from your RV. Imagine yourself a few weeks from now, considerably closer to your tiny life.

ACTION STEP

Set your timer for an hour. Using the Junk Checklist, go through your kitchen and box up for donation or trash the items on the list. Take your donation items from the first three tasks to a donation station and pat yourself on the back for a job well done!

JUNK CHECKLIST - KITCHEN

❑ Single-use gadgets: Garlic/lime press, egg slicer
❑ Mismatched or "one-off" glasses or dishes
❑ To-go containers

❑ Single use plastic bags (RECYCLE THESE PLEASE!)

❑ Old spices (yes, the cologne too!)

❑ Plastic cutlery packets

❑ Old, worn, or extra hand towels

❑ Chipped mugs and dishes

❑ Old jars, vases, pitchers

❑ Excessive cleaning products

❑ Old cookbooks

❑ Take-out menus

❑ Refrigerator magnets

❑ Expired ANYTHING

❑ Duplicates

❑ Specialty platters or dishes you don't use

❑ Tupperware with no lid or lids with no Tupperware

JUNK DRAWER:

❑ Old batteries

❑ Rubber bands

❑ Dried ink pens

❑ Chopsticks

❑ Condiment packets

❑ Mystery keys

❑ Business cards

❑ Coupons

Task 4:
Redd Up from the Bed Up!

It takes 700 gallons of water to make a single cotton shirt.

Some may argue that *Redd* is a Turkish metal-band from the 60s, and they would be correct!

But it's also a Middle English phrase brought to America by the Scottish meaning *to tidy up*. And that's exactly what you're gonna do – you're going to redden up the bedroom!

If you have several bedrooms, you'll attack each one with the same fervor with which you attack your master suite. Your domicile. Your habitación.

Too much?

Listen, I have to make these tasks exciting! BAM! Jump off the page, linguistic gymnastics. And if Middle English phrases and words like *fervor* and *habitación* do the trick... I'm down.

Now, I'll mention what I've said in every task thus far to keep you on track: It's still Section One, and we're just going after the *obvious* "junk."

Now that you've successfully tackled the living room, bathroom, and kitchen, you have a good idea of how it all works.

For this initial run-through of the bedroom, we're going to DONATE or TRASH only.

Grab your bins and your Junk Checklist. The items under attack today are:

- Orphan socks
- Uncomfortable bras
- Old underwear
- Uncomfortable or unworn shoes, sneakers, and boots
- Stretched out or stained t-shirts, dresses, or jeans
- Clothes you haven't worn in 6 months
- Unused purses and gym bags
- Excess hangers

- Kids room: stuffed animals, broken toys, and unused games
- Excess linens, blankets, and seasonal wear
- Ironing boards
- Mismatched or broken jewelry, watches, eyeglasses
- Art that you don't love

This task should be quick – again, about an hour.

Before we finish, I wanna share some statistics:

- 62% of women have clothes in their wardrobe that have *never* been worn
- 83% of women have clothes in their wardrobe that they've only worn once or twice

According to Pareto's Law, we humans only use 20% of our possessions 80% of the time. That means 80% is just sitting around collecting dust. Think about that while you go through these tasks.

Here's another amazing fact: 95% of textiles can be recycled!

In 2018, the EPA estimated that approximately 3.5 million tons of textiles were recycled and therefore, not deposited in landfills. The environmental impact of this number was equivalent to removing over 1.5 million cars from the roads.

You're going through this downsizing process to facilitate a move into a smaller space. You've been working towards and dreaming about a simpler lifestyle. One full of experiences rather than stuff. Now, you're taking the steps to get there.

As we go deeper into your downsizing journey, I think it's important to hear numbers and statistics like these. Not from any political perspective, but a human one. Because you're not only changing the physical space around you, but you're also changing your outlook and your thought process.

Congrats on another successful task completed! Can you believe you're almost through the first section? Damn, that was fast.

Next is the last task of this section. I promise no more Middle English if you promise to stay motivated!

Remember to keep a record of your progress and your process. Go read your WHY. With each passing day, you're a few steps closer to your tiny life!

ACTION STEP

Once again, set your timer for an hour. Put on some mood music and tackle your bedroom using the Junk Checklist. Remember, we're going after the obvious stuff to get rid of, so there should be no emotion here. This should be easy.

JUNK CHECKLIST - BEDROOM

- ❏ Orphan socks
- ❏ Broken Jewelry
- ❏ Unmatched earrings
- ❏ Uncomfortable bras
- ❏ Yellowed, stretched, or stained t-shirts
- ❏ Ill-fitting clothing
- ❏ Worn or old shoes
- ❏ Damaged clothing
- ❏ Excessive winter wear
- ❏ Duplicate items
- ❏ Stuffed animals
- ❏ Clothing not worn in 6 months
- ❏ Damaged eyeglasses
- ❏ Excessive coat hangers
- ❏ Unworn / ill-fitting belts
- ❏ Excessive neckties
- ❏ Damaged watches

Task 5:
Garage Barrage

"It's not hoarding if your shit is cool!"

After this task, section one will be in the books. Your garage may be the single-most challenging downsizing hurdle to get over.

Did you know that 25% of Americans can't even fit a car in their two-car garage?

We spend thousands of dollars on our vehicles. We spend hours maintaining them to keep them in good shape. And then... we park them outside in the elements because our garage is stuffed to capacity with – for the most part – junk.

Maybe you're one of the lucky ones. You're renting and don't have a garage. If this is you, use this task to address your home office, hall closet, or a spare bedroom.

PRO TIP: When downsizing your home office, make sure to shred anything with social security numbers, bank account information, or anything you deem sensitive information.

Some things to look for:

- Old greeting cards that you've kept
- Wrapping paper, ribbons, and tissue paper
- Out of date receipts and business cards
- Old extension cords, calculators, or other obsolete electronics

If you do have a garage, you are not going to stress about this. Breathe in and breathe out. You got this. You've had a lot of practice breaking up with your stuff.

It's still section one. This task is only dealing with the obvious stuff that we've labeled "junk." Grab the Junk Checklist and your bins. Some of the things you're going after are:

- Old rusty tools
- Unused or broken bicycles, scooters, and skateboards
- Old luggage and gym bags
- Broken power tools / cordless tools missing batteries/chargers

- Duplicate tools
- Athletic equipment
- Old paint, paintbrushes, rollers, and chemicals

ATTENTION: You can't simply toss old paint in your trash. While latex paints can be mixed with cat litter, allowed to dry, and then disposed of with your regular trash, oil paints and chemicals such as acetone are considered hazardous materials. They must be handled differently.

Companies like Lowe's and PaintCare accept leftover paint and recycle it. You can also search for a hazardous waste drop-off facility in your area. Or consider donating unused paints rather than throwing them out. Check out:

- **Habitat for Humanity Restores**. The paint will be sold at low rates so even those on a tight budget can do some sprucing up.
- **Global Paint for Charity**. This nonprofit collects used paints and then distributes them to struggling homes, schools, hospitals, and other organizations around the world.
- **Homeless or domestic violence shelters**. Shelters are nearly always strapped for resources and most could make good use of your donated paint.
- **Drama clubs**. Most amateur theater groups operate on a shoestring budget and would be thrilled to get a little free set dressing.

- **Children's charities**. Many nonprofits that work with children would be happy to use your old paint for craft projects.
- **Scout troops**. Scout troops often buy materials for community service projects out of their own pockets. Your donated paint could help their budget go further.

Be proactive and **please don't dump that stuff in the grass or the sewers**. That could be disastrous, not to mention illegal as hell.

So there you have it. The first section is over. Your quest to downsize is in full swing. In section 2 we ramp it up.

I've been where you are. You're probably a little excited and a little freaked out. Experience all of these emotions, and then return to your WHY. I want you to visualize yourself in your new life. Whatever space you've imagined for yourself, put yourself in it right now. See yourself living and thriving in your new uncluttered life.

I know this is not a pipe dream because I've done it. My wife and I downsized from a 1,100-square-foot home with a guest house and shed to a 35-foot sailboat and about 115 square feet. We lived aboard for nearly 6 years and we still had empty cubbies!

Stay focused. Stay motivated. Congratulations!

ACTION STEP

As before, set your timer for an hour. Put on some fun music and tackle your garage using the Junk Checklist. Now look how much better it looks already!

JUNK CHECKLIST - GARAGE

❏ Old rusty tools

❏ Unused or broken bicycles, scooters, and skateboards

❏ Old luggage and gym bags

❏ Broken power tools / cordless tools missing batteries/chargers

❏ Duplicate tools

❏ Athletic equipment

❏ Old paint, paintbrushes, rollers, chemicals, or cleaning supplies

❏ Old cardboard boxes

❏ Oily rags and towels

EXTRA CLOSETS:

❏ Excessive linens / blankets

❏ Electric blankets

❏ Anything cardboard

❏ Shoe boxes / hat boxes

❏ Instruction manuals

❑ Specific seasonal / holiday wear (Ugly Christmas sweaters - outta here!)

❑ Unplayed musical instruments (Donate to a school please!)

❑ Picture frames

❑ Broken / unused tools

❑ Ironing boards

❑ Bags of wrapping paper, ribbons, and fabric

❑ Unused or outdated exercise equipment (Sorry, Thigh Master)

❑ Overnight bags and old luggage

❑ Briefcases

❑ Unused workout clothes

HOME OFFICE:

❑ Stacks of anything

❑ Needless desk ornaments

❑ Unused books or manuals

❑ Old bills / receipts

❑ Calculators

❑ Excessive pens and pencils

❑ Old / outdated electronics

❑ Computer monitors

❑ Extension cords

❑ Chargers you have no idea what they charge

❑ Lamps / chairs / file cabinets

Section 2: Categorize & Sort

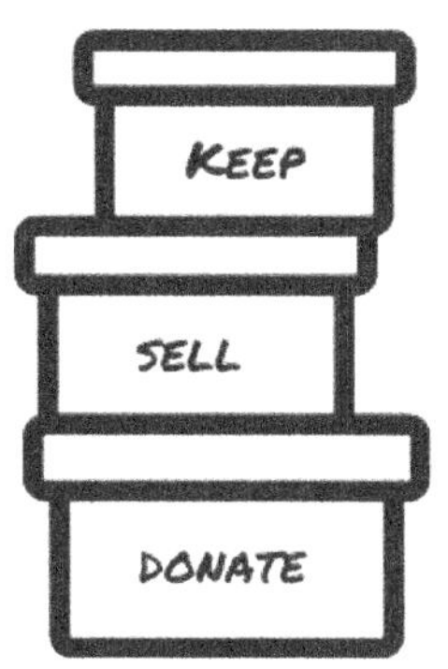

sort

verb / sȯrt /

arrange systematically in groups; separate according to type, class, etc.

Sorting is any process of arranging items systematically, and has two common, yet distinct meanings:
- Ordering: arranging items in a sequence ordered by some criterion
- Categorizing: grouping items with similar properties

In the last section, we tackled the obvious junk. That *should have* been easy. If I were to venture a guess, I'd say you're not missing any of it right now.

This section is like the last one in that you're going to tackle a different room in your home with each task.

These tasks will take a little longer. They might also hurt a little bit.

This is where the psychology of our attachments comes into play. You're going to have to make some tough choices and most likely part with things you've had for a long time.

**Your Mantra for Section 2:
Keep the best. Get rid of the rest!**

Stay focused on the goal. Keep visualizing your tiny life and your future space. Repeat your WHY!

Print the **Room-by-Room Organizer** from the Resource Hub (chrisdicroce.com/tinylife) or get a notebook and make your own (see image below). **You'll need one copy for each room in your house.**

Room-By-Room Organizer			
Room: _______________________________			
Donate	Sell	Keep/Store	Keep for Tiny Life

You'll be going through every item in every room and adding each item to ONE column on this list. Simple.

We've created four categories:

- DONATE: Again, pretty clear (Goodwill, Salvation Army, Veterans, Schools, etc.)
- SELL: Items that have some value and could bring in cash with little effort
- KEEP/STORE: These are items you're keeping but that you'll be storing somewhere
- KEEP/TINY LIFE: These items go with you to your new, simpler life.

Regarding the things in the Keep/Store category: we all have stuff that we just can't get rid of. Maybe something you've had passed to you from deceased parents or friends. Maybe a set of china, sentimental books, or valuable artwork. These things are important to you and no, they shouldn't be classified as junk or disposable.

These are the items you're going to have to find a way to store.

Basically, for these items, you have two options:

- Ask a family member or friend who has extra room in their home to hang onto it for you
- Rent a storage unit

I recommend the first option if at all possible because I think storage units are a waste of money and add undue stress.

There are other drawbacks to having a storage unit, too.

STORAGE UNITS = Deferred Decisions x Stress

When you store your stuff, you're creating a future task. At some point, you have to deal with that storage unit. That creates stress. We're trying to minimize stress and free your mind.

Read more about why I hate storage units in this article: www.savingtosail.com/the-downsizing-secret-that-could-save-you-1200-a-year

If you have no other choice but to rent a storage unit, depending on your tiny living situation, you may want to make sure that someone you trust has access for many reasons besides an emergency. For example, you might need to send something home to be stored or have something shipped from your unit to you wherever you might be traveling.

It's also a great idea to have an additional point of contact in case the storage facility needs to reach you but can't. This can happen if you're on a boat in a remote anchorage with no wifi. Trust me... this happens. It's good to be prepared.

When you're finished with Section 2, you'll have several designated stacks. And they may be big stacks. But each one will be clearly labeled, and you'll know *exactly* where it's going. There'll be no guesswork and therefore, no stress.

GOLF CLUBS OR GULF CLUBS?

Task 1:
Sorting Your Bitchin' Kitchen

"Cleanliness is next to impossible."
-New Adventures of Winnie The Pooh

This entire section is geared toward getting organized, categorizing, and sorting. Today, we go back to the kitchen.

Remember your mantra for Section 2: Keep the best. Get rid of the rest!

Over the years, things tend to add up. When we tackled our kitchen, we found two crockpots and two blenders, along with a host of other duplicates and mismatched items.

So, where do you even begin in the kitchen? You begin with:

Duplicates & Multiples

- Roasting pans & baking sheets
- Stockpots, skillets, soup pans
- Strainers & colanders
- Drinking glasses, wine glasses, & coffee mugs
- Excess Tupperware: keep the ones with the best seals
- Mixing bowls & large cutting boards
- Serving platters & large decorative salad bowls

Take the highest quality, most versatile items to your new tiny home. Sell or donate the rest.

Every day is a good day: Do away with the *good dishes* vs. *everyday dishes* mentality immediately.

I've never understood the compulsion to have a cabinet full of ornate dishes that get used maybe once a year. Keep a nice set of plain white dishes or something you know you'll use. An elegant cloth napkin and placemat will take it up a notch for a more formal presentation.

While it may be tempting, resist the urge to have plastic *everything* in your new life, even if you're on a boat. Trust me, at the end of the day, sipping a nice wine from a real glass or piece of stemware goes a long way towards making you feel human. Nobody wants to drink a lovely Malbec that tastes like plastic.

If you have valuable china that you must keep, you probably won't be bringing that to your tiny home so add that to the KEEP/STORE list.

Pantry Raid!

- Toss old spices & bags of flour – if they're still good, give 'em to a neighbor.
- Recycle your single-use plastic bags.
- Pare down excessive mops, brooms, & dust-busters.
- What's under your sink? Get rid of excess cleaning products and sponges.

Single-Use & Specialty Items

- If you have a traditional blender and an immersion blender, keep the immersion blender for your new home. It's much more manageable space-wise. If you're in a boat or RV, you'll probably need an inverter to use it.
- Coffee makers: These days, a French Press (we like the double-walled stainless version) or an <u>AeroPress</u> makes a great cup of coffee, takes up less space, and uses *no power*. We love our AeroPress!
- Mixers, food processors, and juicers are tough sells in a small space. See: **The Power Issue** below.
- Go manual. Hand operated coffee grinders work well and use no power.

THE POWER ISSUE

Living on a boat or in an RV not only presents challenges related to space and storage, but it also presents additional challenges when it comes to powering them all. If you're moving to a tiny house and will be connected to the grid, power might not be the issue. It will be more about the real estate these items occupy. Counter and cabinet space are at a premium no matter what tiny platform you live in.

Unless you're plugged into a power pedestal, you'll be using DC (battery) power. None of your conventional kitchen appliances will run on DC power.

If you want to use that immersion blender on the hook or in the RV park, you'll need an inverter. This isn't a big deal but know what size you need to run those appliances. And you should know that inverters also drain precious battery power.

Everyone is going to be different here. You may have a gourmet kitchen full of beautiful, high-quality, expensive cookware. Downsizing your kitchen may require more time and energy but the tactics and principles are the same. You just may need to do it a few times to get where you want to be.

Selling my 30-quart All-Clad stockpot along with the rest of my specialty cookware on Craigslist broke my heart. But they were never going to work on my boat. I sold them for a great price and added those extra dollars to our mason jar.

Visualizing the bigger picture helps from here on out.

Congratulations. I know this task was a difficult one. If you think you need to take a second run at your kitchen space, don't stress about it. Do it as many times as you need.

ACTION STEP

Print your **Room-by-Room Organizer** from the Resource Hub (<u>chrisdicroce.com/tinylife</u>) or create your own, label it "Kitchen" and grab your bins! Go through every item in your kitchen and write it on the appropriate column on your sheet. Once you've allocated an item to a column, put it in its designated bin.

Room-By-Room Organizer			
Room: ______________________			
Donate	Sell	Keep/Store	Keep for Tiny Life
_______	_______	_______	_______
_______	_______	_______	_______
_______	_______	_______	_______
_______	_______	_______	_______
_______	_______	_______	_______
_______	_______	_______	_______

Task 2:
Whittling Down Your Wardrobe

In this task, we tackle your wardrobe. In section one, you got rid of your stretched out, old Fruit of the Looms and the underwire bras that poked you in the ribs. In other words, the easy stuff.

Now, it's time to go after that gorgeous dress you bought in Soho but have yet to remove the tags. Gentlemen, that purple pinstripe shirt that you wear once every three years and those hushpuppies from 1981 are in grave danger.

In this task, we're paring everything down to the items you wear most. Everything else, we're viewing as expendable.

When we're done, the only things left in your closet will be things you **love** and **wear**.

In case you've been living in a bubble or under a rock and never heard of it before, let me introduce you to the **CAPSULE WARDROBE** concept.

Creating a **Capsule Wardrobe** means paring down to a mini wardrobe made up of high-use versatile pieces that can be mixed and matched with each other to create several different outfits.

There are countless examples of capsules to be found online, but the one thing that runs pretty consistently through all of them is the estimate of just how many pieces of clothing we actually use. That number is somewhere between 30 and 40. Yep, that's it.

You might be saying, "What! No way I'm doing that!" If you remember that we only wear 20% of everything we own, this amount makes perfect sense. But, let me try to make this a little easier.

Of course, it's going to be incredibly difficult for me to design your wardrobe, not knowing your location, travel plans, or if you'll be working a job that requires actual work attire, but I'm going to try.

LET'S BREAK IT DOWN!

Clean and Sort: Pull everything out of your closet and lay it on the bed.

Then separate that pile into 3 smaller piles.

YES:
- Things you absolutely love and want to keep
- Shoes that are comfortable and get worn
- Things you view as irreplaceable

NO:
- Haven't worn it in the last six months (or ever)
- Tags still attached

MAYBE: This one is on you.
- If it's something you hope to someday fit into, get rid of it. That creates future stress.
- If it's something you love because of the color or print, but don't wear it often, it's a maybe.

What to Keep:

- Work clothes (if applicable) or clothes that are needed for special meetings
- Pants or jeans that can be worn with multiple tops, sweaters, & blazers
- Jackets and sweaters that can be mixed, matched & worn through multiple seasons
- Tops that are versatile enough to go with several items (pants, jeans, skirts)

- Shoes that can be worn with multiple outfits
- Scarves that you can use to dress up a casual outfit

Summer wear will be light and easily mixed and matched. It might look like this:

- Jeans
- (2) pairs of shorts
- Casual dress pants
- Sundresses
- Flip flops, sandals, sneakers
- Tank tops
- Bathing suit

Winter wear might include:

- Tank tops from summer (used as a base layer)
- A few sweaters
- Jeans from your summer capsule
- Leggings
- Heavier Jacket
- Boots
- Scarves
- Hat

One way to make it easier is to hold onto more neutral items or pieces of clothing that aren't too trendy. Have a base of neutral colors, then pick one or two colors that you like and look good in to add some variety.

Then use scarves or accessories as your accent pieces to dress things up a little. (A colorful printed scarf can go a long way with a white t-shirt and jeans) This will also extend the life of your wardrobe, as the majority of your pieces will be timeless.

Again, this is going to be an individual puzzle that only you know the answer to. But as you can see from the two lists above, we've got two capsules started with a total of 15 items. There's room for another 20!

Workout clothing, underwear, and accessories (watches, belts, earrings, scarves), don't count towards your final number.

Now, put that **MAYBE** pile somewhere out of sight. If you don't remember what's in there after a month, don't look at it or go through it again. Just load it into the car and donate it.

And there's one more rule. It's the most important one. **Don't buy *anything* new!**

For this to work, you have to stop buying stuff. Don't fill your hard-won space with new stuff. Stay the course and resist the urge to buy something unless you absolutely need it.

Creating your Capsule Wardrobe doesn't just create space. It alleviates stress in two ways:

- No more decision fatigue

- No more choice overload

By creating a Capsule Wardrobe, you reduced the number of decisions you have to make and drastically reduced the number of choices you have.

Not convinced?

Remember Steve Jobs? He wore his signature black sweater and jeans every day. He said by doing that, he had one less decision to make. He knew exactly what he was wearing every single day. Who's gonna argue with his success? Not me.

It's been proven that once you exercise your willpower to make a tough choice, it's easier to make that choice the next time.

PRO TIP: If you're not sure about this whole Capsule Wardrobe thing, try this method for two weeks: Hang all of your clothes in the closet with the hangers facing the same way. Whenever you wear an item, hang it up with the hanger facing the opposite way. After a couple of weeks, you'll know exactly what you've worn and what you haven't.

Fun Fact: You wear only 20% of your clothes 80% of the time.

Now, I want you to celebrate your wins. I know this sounds like a bunch of wispy, new-age crap. But If you chose 37 as the number of items you wanted to keep and you hit it, celebrate! If you chose 50 as your number and it's still significantly less than what you started with, I'll consider that a win too.

- Have a martini
- Have a shot of tequila (Go easy with this one, soldier. You still have a lot to get done.)
- Go out to dinner
- Grab a great bottle of wine
- Have a seltzer!

Do whatever it is you do to celebrate, EXCEPT go shopping.

This was a difficult task, but you did it. That's what I'm telling myself as I write my closing here. This is where I ask you to remember the big picture again. Visualize yourself living the life you've imagined.

Thanks for hanging in there. Tackling the kitchen and your wardrobe is huge! By now, you should be getting the hang of this.

ACTION STEP

Create your capsule wardrobe! Pile every item in your wardrobe on your bed and go through each item, designating it as YES, NO, or MAYBE. NO items get re-sorted into DONATE or SELL bins. MAYBE items go into a box. If you haven't accessed anything in the box after one month, donate it.

Task 3:
The Whole Enchilada

"When you get tired, learn to rest.
Not to quit."
-Banksy

To get to this point, you've done some serious work. I've challenged you to rethink, reprogram and reorganize, and here you are.

You've made it this far and I don't need to wax philosophic about your new future anymore. It's game on. You have a clear goal directly in front of you and the tools with which to achieve that goal. From here on out, you only need to ask yourself one question when it comes to an item:

Does this fit in my new life?

Task 3 is all about applying the techniques you've learned thus far to the rest of your house.

- Kids rooms
- Guest rooms
- Home office
- Garage
- Attic
- Basement

Using the **Junk Checklist** in conjunction with your **Room-by-Room Organizer**, go through each room, garage, attic, and basement... the whole enchilada.

This will be the second time through these rooms. The first time was just the junk. Be ruthless. Be honest with yourself.

As we go even deeper into this process, some serious soul-searching is going to have to occur. Let's face it, the junk was easy. How hard was it to throw away those dried-up cans of paint in the garage? Probably not very hard.

This task will take you longer as you move from room to room.

At the end of this task, every item in your home should be listed on the **Room-by-Room Organizer**. It's going to be in one of 4 columns:

- DONATE
- SELL
- KEEP/STORE
- KEEP FOR TINY LIFE

If it's not listed in one of the above categories, it's TRASH.

As you become less emotional about your stuff, what you once thought was irreplaceable becomes trash pretty quickly. And that's when things start to get fun!

SIZE MATTERS

I talked earlier about the negative returns associated with storage units. I wanna talk about this a bit more as it pertains to the bigger items that you may be tempted to store, like washers and dryers, refrigerators, big-screen TVs, and furniture.

It directly correlates to the Psychology of Stuff I mentioned way back in the beginning.
We tend to over-value our stuff, remember? *The Endowment Effect* and the *Sunk-Cost Bias* will rear their ugly heads and scream bloody murder during this task. You need to ignore them!

You can't keep an itemized list in your head about "what you're losing" when you tackle this task. If you do, you'll fail. You must instead:

- Forget what you paid for the items you're getting rid of. It's irrelevant. (Remember the truth about retail markups I mentioned in The Psychology of Stuff?)
- Focus on your new tiny life and what you'll be gaining
- Focus on living with less stress
- Focus on having more time. More freedom. More money.

I said earlier that I recommend paying for a storage unit only as a last resort. Let me expand a bit on why I say this.

Storing that washer and dryer is going to cost you a significant amount of money.

When you pay to store these types of items, you're paying to store what I call *diminishing technology*. Each year, technology tops itself. That washer and dryer will be virtually obsolete in about 2 years. If it's not, it will be woefully inefficient compared to the newer models.

New efficient washing machines use 13 gallons of water compared to conventional ones which can use up to 23 gallons. What will that difference be in two years?

Refrigerators manufactured after the year 2000 use up to 60% less energy. Here's a little perspective. In the 1970s, refrigerators used a whopping 2200 kWh (kilowatt-hour) of energy per year. By the early '90s, that number dropped to around 1100 kWh. In the mid-

2000s, it fell to around 600 kWh per year and now we're closer to 300 kWh on the most efficient models. Some are predicting we could be looking a 150 kWh per year in the near future.

What's it all mean?

Five years from now, newer appliances are going to be twice as efficient with their power and water usage. If you pay for storage in order to keep these appliances, you'll have spent money to keep antiquated items that you're ultimately going to replace anyway. The storage fees alone will amount to several times the cost of replacement appliances.

These items will never be worth more than they are right now. Sell them!

Worth Mentioning: If you're selling your home, some of these items might have to remain with your house. Check with your listing agent before you donate or sell anything!

CAR TALK

Assessing your vehicles is hard to do without knowing where you live and what your work situation is.

- Do you live in a city with reliable public transportation?
- Do you have kids that need to go to daycare/school/events?

- Will you be living aboard at a marina and need a car for transportation?
- Are you still attaching your identity to your car?

I just threw that last one in to see if you were paying attention.

Here's how we handled downsizing our vehicles before moving onto a boat in 2012.

We owned two: a 2002 VW Passat and a 2000 Ford Ranger pick-up truck, both paid off. We were debt-free and totally against car payments. Cars were simply tools for us.

Several months before realizing our dream of leaving Nashville and heading to the boat in Fort Lauderdale, Florida, we gave Melody's car to her mom. We did with one vehicle for about 4 months. It was a challenge, but it was also fun sharing our morning drive to work.

Being that I had some freelance work waiting for me in Fort Lauderdale, we kept the truck because I thought having at least one vehicle would make it easier, and at first, it did. Having a way to get around and go shopping for groceries was nice. But hanging onto my truck quickly became a bit of a nightmare.

When we left Lauderdale to sail north for hurricane season, I had to find a place to park it until we arrived at our next location on the Chesapeake Bay. That usually meant a marina. And marinas charge for everything.

Once we arrived up north, I had to fly back to Fort Lauderdale to get the truck. In the fall we reversed the process. After a couple of seasons of doing this, we sold the truck. I found a cheap, second-hand bike that worked great for our needs moving forward.

These days, Uber and Lyft are everywhere. If the weather isn't cooperating with your bike ride or walk to the market, Uber is pretty cheap and readily available. With the money you're saving not having to pay for gas or car insurance, these car services shouldn't cause too much pain. Melody and I even used Uber to get around in Guatemala!

If you're moving onto a boat, your car situation is gonna require some thought and reflection on your end. For us, doing away with the maintenance costs, insurance, and worrying far outweighed the convenience it provided.

So, here's a quick recap for Task 3.

- Sort and categorize each item in the rest of your house
- Decide what to do with the big items (appliances, cars, etc.)
- Think long and hard about every item you place in the KEEP/STORE column
- Then... think again about every item you've placed in the KEEP/STORE column

This is a big one. Don't get discouraged or overwhelmed. Take your time and remember that this isn't a race. Be diligent and don't stress. If you're unsure about an item, put it in a column. You can always change it later.

When you finish this task, you will be so much closer to achieving your dream of living on your sailboat, traveling in your RV, or living simply in your tiny house! Good luck.

ACTION STEP

Print the **Room-by-Room Organizer** from the Resource Hub (<u>chrisdicroce.com/tinylife</u>) or create your own. You'll need one for each room in the rest of the house. Now grab your bins and one-by-one, go through every other room in your house, repeating the steps from Task 1 from this section.

Room-By-Room Organizer

Room: _______________________________

Donate	Sell	Keep/Store	Keep for Tiny Life

Task 4:
The Great Pretender

*"Life is just a bunch of short stories
pretending to be a novel."*
-Unknown

Hey! How are you feeling? Mad at me yet? I completely understand. This is difficult but worth it.

Task 3 was a major undertaking, but you should now have everything that you own categorized and designated to a specific pile. The big, heavy stuff can stay where it is for a little while longer.

The smaller stuff, you should've placed in your bins. You know what you're keeping, what you're selling and donating, and what you're taking with you to your tiny home. No more guesswork!

Here in Task 4, we're going to focus on the items in the two columns labeled: KEEP/STORE and KEEP FOR TINY LIFE.

- **For the next week, you are only allowed to use/live with items you packed into the KEEP FOR TINY LIFE column.**

These are the items you deliberately set aside to take with you for your tiny life and now, you're going to see how well you chose.

All the other bins (*the ones you've labeled, KEEP/STORE, DONATE, and SELL*) get stashed out of sight in the garage or a spare room. For the next week, you're going to *pretend* this stuff is already gone.

Should you find, during this week, that you need something from the other bins, go ahead and grab it. Please, exercise some self-control here. The only reason you're keeping this stuff at all is to make sure you don't get rid of something prematurely.

And this exercise works both ways.

If at the end of this task, you find that there were things in the KEEP FOR TINY LIFE bin that you never touched, you might want to rethink their necessity and exile them to the DONATE or SELL bins.

So there it is. Task 4 is all about pretending. Do your best not to raid the bins you've stashed. Out of sight, out of mind. I'd venture to say, you'll do just fine with the stuff you've picked. Who knows, you might even toss some of what you thought you needed into the SELL or DONATE bins.

This exercise may sound silly, but you'd be surprised at how much people keep and carry into their new Tiny Life only to realize they brought too much.

A prime example: one reader was so enthusiastic at how well she had done with her downsizing to move onto her boat.

She and her husband loaded up their Suburban with their boat pile and found that when they got to their boat to move aboard, not all of it would fit! So they had to downsize yet again... on the dock!

ACTION STEP

For one full week, use ONLY items you listed into the KEEP FOR TINY LIFE column of your Room-by-Room Organizer. If you must access something that was designated in one of the other columns, decide whether it's an actual need and if so, consider bringing it with you in your new Tiny Life. If you have items left over from your TINY LIFE column that you didn't use, consider selling or donating them.

Task 5:
The Price Is Right

Here we are in the last task of Section 2. You're halfway there! In Task 5, we're going to do a bit of prep work so that when Section 3 kicks off, which is all about selling, you'll hit the ground running.

Gather up those Room-by-Room Organizer sheets from earlier in the section. Now, transfer each item in the SELL column onto the **Price Sheet** located in the Resource Hub (chrisdicroce.com/tinylife) or create your own as shown at the end of this task.

- Washer and Dryer
- Refrigerator
- Living Room Furniture: Be specific. Break it down (Couch, Coffee Table)
- Television
- Bedroom sets: Again, be specific

- End tables and desks
- Kitchen table
- Lamps and large mirrors
- Rugs
- Cars, boats, big toys

On the Price Sheet, you'll notice three columns:

- **What It's Worth (for real):** Do a quick search on Craigslist or Facebook Marketplace to see what similar items are selling for. I know this is an added step, but by seeing what other items are going for, you avoid the trappings of *The Endowment Effect* and don't overprice the item.

- **What I Want:** This is the price you want to get for your item. Resist the urge to over-inflate the cost *just because you own it*. Be realistic. Sell it fast. Positive reinforcement.

- **What I'll Accept:** This is the lowest price you'll accept. By determining this beforehand and writing it down, it eliminates the need to remember it or have to think about it if someone makes you a lower offer than your listed price. Instead, it's right there in front of you, the lowest price you'll accept. No thinking. No remembering. No searching for it.

When you begin listing and selling, this sheet will be a huge time and stress saver. Trust me.

So get started, and before moving on to Section 3 (which will show you effective ways to sell your items), you'll need to fully complete this task.

ACTION STEP
Gather up those **Room-by-Room Organizer sheets** from earlier in the section. Now, transfer each item in the SELL column onto the Price Sheet located in the Resource Hub (<u>chrisdicroce.com/tinylife</u>) or create your own as shown below.

Price Sheet

Item	What It's Worth	What I Want	What I'll Accept

Section 3:
Sell Baby Sell

This section is all about the sale. You've done the hard work of trashing, sorting, and separating, it's time to discuss *how* we're gonna trade it for dollars.

Many of us think eBay and Craigslist are the only games in town when it comes to selling. They're not. The game has changed.

In this section, I'm going to:

- Give you 8 great alternatives to eBay & Craigslist
- Tell you why I don't recommend eBay for selling your stuff
- Show you how to create killer ads that get a response

- Show you how to take great photos & present your items in the *best light* (cough, cough)
- Reveal my favorite gadget for increasing your sales
- Tell you why you *never* want to have a garage sale

Are you ready? Excited? Can you feel the warm sand on your feet, the salt spray on your lips?
Do your family and friends think you're nuts? Are your neighbors worried about you? Good!

That means you've been stirring it up. Making a mess. You've probably had a few heated discussions with your partner as well. I know we did! Downsizing doesn't just affect your life. It affects those around you, too.

Now is a great time to talk about how all of this change impacts the people close to you.

Right about now, everyone in your circle is probably expressing grave concerns about what you're doing. I remember some of our friends and family approached us and jokingly said, "Are you dying?"

The ones who truly love you and want you to be happy will be inspired by your upcoming life change. So much so, they might make a few changes themselves. They'll be the ones you need to lean on now. You'll need their help once you start selling.

Other people will shrug off this "downsizing nonsense" *until* you sell off your "prized possessions." Once that happens, they may start acting really weird. And that's because they may feel a little bit threatened by all of your big changes.

It's called *Social Undermining*. I know, it sounds crazy, but it's true.

But hey, cut these folks some slack. They don't have the newfound enlightenment that you have. They may not understand the psychology of stuff the way you do. You have a bigger picture in mind. Focus on that. Don't let anyone steal your joy or hijack your progress with their negativity.

Okay... I got the heavy crap out of the way. Some of this stuff ain't fun, but I think it's important. Having more information and better understanding is never a bad thing.

Now let's go make some money!

Task 1:
Get a Gadget! Got It?

"Being a square keeps you from going around in circles."
-J Vernon McGee

How ya doing at this point?

Are you able to sneak in a bit of daydreaming? In addition to all of the information and tasks in these sections, you're still juggling *regular life* stuff. Things need to get done. I know when I went through the process, it was all-encompassing. My dog was looking at me as though he felt he was next to go.

You're probably a little overwhelmed right now. And my bad humor probably isn't helping either. So let's make this easy. This task isn't a task at all. It's more of a... tip.

A downsizing hack that can help make things a little smoother.

In the overview, I said I was going to let you in on a fancy little gadget that will help you increase profits when it came time to sell your items. It's time.

Meet the Square.

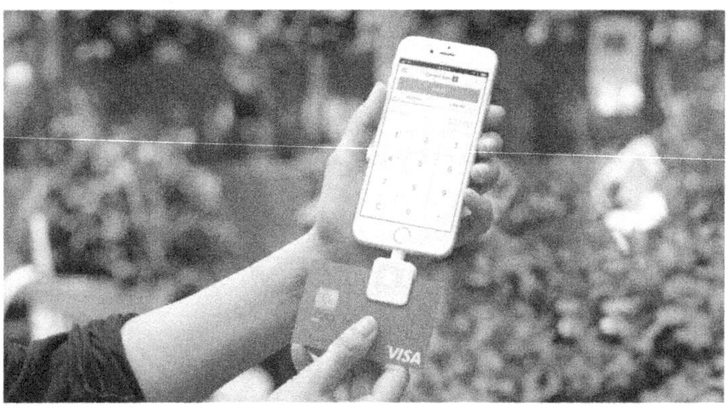

Maybe you know it, maybe you don't. But this little device turns your phone or tablet into a cash register.

- Plug it into your phone or tablet
- Swipe the buyer's debit or credit card
- Get a signature (They can use their fingernail)

You're done. They get an emailed receipt, and you get paid.

How do you get one?

Simply go to the Square website (squareup.com) and sign up for an account. They'll mail you the mag strip reading device *for free*. They charge a small merchant fee per transaction and it can vary depending on the transaction (at the time of this publishing, ~2.75%).

Here's why I like this thing.

- No monthly fees
- No hidden fees
- Deposits usually post to your bank account in 2 business days
- They offer full chargeback protection and payment dispute assistance

You may be asking yourself, "Why in the world do I need this thing?"

Because you want to make it incredibly easy for buyers to give you money and walk away with the item they purchased.

> The excuse: *"I would love to buy this, but I didn't bring cash."*
> The response: *"No problem. I can take a card."*
> BAM!

So – if you think you're ready to enter the SELL phase, which is next, your assignment is to get online and order a Square card reader.

ACTION STEP

Go to squareup.com, set up an account, and order a card reader. The magstripe reader for your phone is free. Thank me later.

Task 2:
Online Marketplaces

"There's more than one way to sell a couch."

As mentioned in the section overview, this section is all about the sale. I'm going to show you how to take great photos, write strong copy that gets noticed, and post it where people will see it.

I'll cover the entire process, but first, I want to talk about the options available to you now that you're ready to sell your items. I mentioned that I don't like eBay (for this) and here's why.

When you sell something on eBay, 99% of the time it will require you to ship the item. That requires you to find a box, pack the item securely, and make a trip to the post office or UPS or FedEx. This is creating much more work.

I'm trying to save you work.

Yes, eBay is an awesome resource, but not for this specific exercise. For this, we want a local buyer who comes to you, gives you some dollars and drives away with the item. Done.

And that brings me to Craigslist. I'm sure you're aware of it, whether you've used it or not. It's a great tool for selling your items locally because it's free and it's recognizable. Everyone knows about Craigslist. But it's not without its faults.

It has its share of shady people. You have to be aware of the scammers. Unfortunately, that's the part of selling none of us like. Today, there are some great alternatives. Some you know and some you don't.

8 GREAT ALTERNATIVES TO CRAIGSLIST

Facebook Marketplace: Facebook is huge. Its Orwellian presence can't be overstated. And, while I've grown quite tired of cat pictures and political discord, I have to admit, Facebook Marketplace is a great tool for selling your items locally, and just like Craigslist, it's free! Also, just like Craigslist, keep your eye out for scammers.

Letgo: You may not have heard about this app available on iPhone, but it's probably the most popular alternative to Craigslist right now. I like it because it does a little better job of letting you categorize your items into specific groups like fashion, home and garden, etc. Letgo is a little safer, too. To get an account, the user must verify their Google or Facebook profile. Additionally, communicating through the Letgo app keeps you from having to list your phone number or email. That's a huge plus.

Recycler (recycler.com): With over 18 million users, Recycler lets you sell anything and everything you could sell on Craigslist. You can quickly share your listing on your Facebook and Twitter feeds as well as boost your visibility with paid ads.

Offerup (offerup.com): Although much smaller than the others on this list, Offerup lets you operate via the smartphone app and broadcast your listings on Facebook. Similar to Craigslist, Offerup differentiates itself by letting both buyers and sellers receive ratings, which can make the process feel a little more secure, and it keeps the scammers at bay. If someone is interested in your item, they can either accept your list price or, like the name says, make you an offer.

Bookoo (bookoo.com): As in "bookoo bucks!" This is a smaller "family-friendly" (for lack of a better term) alternative to Craigslist. This site used to be more prevalent in military towns to assist young families moving in and out more frequently. Now, it can be found everywhere. You do have to create a user profile (which is free) and that's why I like it. Making people create a profile before they can sell weeds out the scammers (in my mind anyway).

Poshmark (poshmark.com): This is a great app-based marketplace similar to Craigslist, but **specifically for fashion: clothes, shoes, jewelry, accessories, and handbags**. You use the site's free app to list items, and when someone makes a purchase, you get a prepaid shipping label to mail the item.

Geebo (geebo.com): If you live in a major metropolitan area like Denver, Chicago, or L.A. this might be the way to go. Geebo offers users what they call "Safe Trade Transactions." This is where the buyer and seller agree to formalize the transaction at a local police department. Sounds strange, but for those concerned with safety, isn't it better than exchanging money in some McDonald's parking lot?

Gazelle (gazelle.com): This site is mainly for selling your electronics, such as old smartphones, iPads, video games, and more. It isn't locally based, but the great thing about it is that when someone buys your item, Gazelle gives you a free shipping label to print. Just box your item up, stick on the label, and hand it to the mailman.

If you have something and you want to sell it, there's a way to do it. I could have listed ten more sites that make it possible to sell your stuff, but I don't want to overwhelm you with too many choices. Chances are, ten minutes after I publish this book, some of these will disappear but fear not, a dozen others will appear in their place.

I love the idea of broadcasting items on Facebook and communicating via a phone app rather than by listing your personal phone number or email. I would take advantage of the sites that allow you to do it that way.

In the next task, we're going to tap into your inner Ansel Adams. Lights! Camera! Wait... don't scream *action* yet. You'll scare the neighbors. We'll do that in Section 3 when I show you how to take clicks that *get* clicked!

ACTION STEP

Look at the several options I share for selling your belongings and choose which one works best for you. You can totally use more than one.

Task 3:
Every Picture Tells A Story

When it comes to your listing photo:
less bad is better.

Shazam!

We've all seen the ads. A cluttered, blurry photo. Too much or not enough light. It *looks* like a sofa, but you can't be certain. There's an old blanket, maybe some food, a pair of underwear sticking out from under a cushion... possibly some offensive text.

Don't believe me? Check out this REAL ad I found. Scary isn't the word!

FREE COUCH .. sits three normal folks, six kids, or two fatties with snacks in the middle. Each end is a recliner, that really recline. Brown, stained. and from dirty house with cat hair and smoke. Comfy as all hell .. STONERS PARADISE.

You come get it. It's heavy as f*uck, so bring some strong dudes or a few butchy gals.

Please note: Woman not included. You don't want her anyway. She hasn't had her coffee yet. You may keep whatever whoever you find in the couch.
* * * * * *
6 11 15 $10 to whoever comes and gets this beast. The couch .. not her.

It's FREE. And he's offering $10.00 if you go get it! Would you do it? Me either.

People underestimate the effect a photo can have on a sale. "Just point and shoot." Isn't that what the old Canon commercial said? I guess that works if you're famed photog Annie Leibovitz, but for the rest of us, it's not that simple.

Quality photos get more attention. When your photos are clear, in focus, and uncluttered (just like your new life). people will be more likely to click on your ad.

Don't go buy a fancy camera. Modern smartphones are *more* than capable of taking good quality photos that clearly display what you're selling.

So, how does one take a great photo? Let's use that living room sofa I joked about. You can start by:

- Making sure it's clean! Buy some upholstery cleaner and deal with any glaring stains
- Vacuuming up any pet hair. Make sure to get under the cushions
- Repairing any defects, like crooked or loose legs
- Removing anything in the photo that isn't included in the sale
- Moving the sofa if you have to, so you can get a nicer photo with better lighting

If you need to pull that couch into the middle of the room so the natural light from your large picture window hits it, do it. Here's a good example I found on Craigslist. This photo is crisp. The lighting is good enough. Prospective buyers have a pretty clear idea of its condition just from this one photo.

Don't go crazy. Don't spend hours on a few pictures but do spend a few minutes to make sure you get a good image. Snap 30 photos if you must.

How to take great photos:

- Hold your camera sideways or in the landscape orientation.
- Don't shoot the item straight on. Give it some dimension by shooting it at an angle
- Don't get too close or too far away. Try to fill the frame with the object
- If it has something special or unique, capture that in a close-up
- Use natural light if you can. Windows or patio doors are better than overhead lighting
- If you can take the object outside, shoot it in the soft morning or late afternoon light
- Avoid shooting outside between the hours of 11am – 3pm when the sun is directly overhead

When taking photos of clothing, you can approach this one of two ways. Put the outfit on to show how it fits your body or lay the outfit neatly on the bed. Avoid busy patterns that detract from your items.

The best option is always to show the dress or pants on, so the person who's buying it can see the item. If you do this:
- Shoot the photo from the neck down.
- Avoid faces, especially kids.

There's no need to see the face of the person who's modeling. Remember, it's the internet.

PRO TIP: Set aside one full day (or however many hours you believe you'll need) to take photos. The couch, the bedroom set, the washer and dryer, and so-on.

Create a file on your desktop and label it To Sell. Now, do one big import of all your images, and you're ready to go. Once you have photos of each item that you plan to sell, try to list them all at the same time.

Doing it this way is more efficient than taking photos of one item, downloading those photos, listing the item, and then going back to take more photos of your other items. That can be a bit daunting.

- Set aside one day for photo taking
- Download all your photos at once
- Do multiple listings to save time

You're a step closer to seeing some cold hard cash replace that dusty old couch. And that gets you another step closer to your simpler, tinier life.

ACTION STEP

Set aside a day to take photos of all your "to sell" items. Create a folder on your computer labeled "To Sell". Import all of your photos from the day and label them so they're easy to find.

Task 4:
It Ain't Gonna Sell Itself!

We've got a lot to cover here, so I'm going to dispense with my kooky humor and witty banter and get right into it. Today, I'm going to show you how to write a listing that gets noticed.

For demonstration purposes, I'm going to use Craigslist in this task, but this listing tactic will work wherever you decide to list your items. And I do suggest multiple listings. The more people that see your ad, the better the chances and the quicker the results. Obvious, right?

So, why do some people sell a ton of stuff, seemingly without effort, while others never get a single email? It all comes down to how your ad looks *and* how it reads.

The ads on Craigslist use the same format. That's a good thing for you. You don't have to pick fonts, colors, or templates. And it's super easy.

If you've never used it, visit Craigslist.org and take a look. Once you click your location, you'll see the main categories and sub-categories.

First, you'll log in or *create a new account* if you don't have one. Once you sign into your account:

- Click **New Posting**
- Select your city's location
- Select Posting Type: **for sale by owner**
- Select your category: **furniture - by owner**
- Choose locale: Your County

Once you're through with that, this is what the listing page will look like.

posting title   price specific location postal code

posting body

posting details

make / manufacturer   model name / number   size / dimensions

language of posting condition

english

cryptocurrency ok include "more ads by this user" link

contact info

email

CL mail relay (recommended)
no replies to this email

users can also contact me:

  by phone by text   phone number extension contact name

show on maps

street optional

cross street optional

city

ok for others to contact you about other services, products or commercial interests

continue

It's all very self-explanatory. If you try to post without having the information required, it will prompt you to complete the form. You can set your preferred means of contact and whether or not you want a map to accompany the listing.

You have very little space to make a big impact. What makes the impact? Your *photo* and the accompanying *Posting Title.*

You might be the Ernest Hemingway of Craigslist. Your prose might make people weep. But if they never click the ad, they'll never read your prose. Thusly, never weep. Feel me?

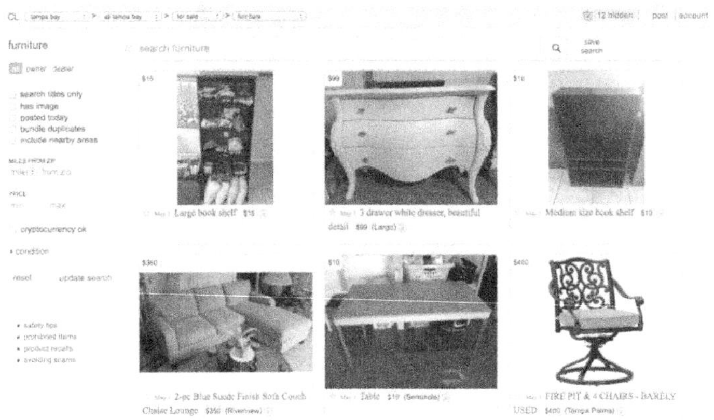

Let's use a real listing for the sofa above as our example. We'll walk through this listing step by step, starting with the headline.

2-pc Blue Suede Finish Sofa Couch Chaise Lounge $350.00 (Riverview)

Because the headline contains the words Sofa, Couch, *and* Chaise Lounge, it will show up in several searches. If someone happens to just type Chaise Lounge in their search box, this listing will come up. That's good!

This headline also tells me several things immediately. It's a 2-piece set. It's Blue. And, it's suede.

Your headline should give the most important details in a succinct, clear way. The only thing that could make this headline better is if it told me something about the condition.

Example: Like New 2-pc Blue Suede Sofa, Couch, Chaise Lounge $350.00 (Riverview)

The Posting Body: This is just a fancy way of saying *Description.*

The general rule here is: Explain the features and benefits in as few words as possible so that they satisfy the potential buyers' need to know. "How much is too much," you ask?

Well, it depends. If you're selling a car, you may have a long list of modifications and updates. If you're selling a chair, you won't. It's a chair. The listing might include materials it's made from and the dimensions.

Let's look at that Blue Suede Sofa / Couch / Chaise Lounge listing once again.

7.5-foot sofa/chaise covered in light blue suede finish fabric.
Made by H. M. Richards at HMRichards.com.
Beautiful, near new condition. lightly used.
Kept on glassed-in lanai under dust cover.

The sectional features seat cushions, loose stuffed pillow backs and an elongated cushion and movable base to create a chaise, which can be used on either the right or left side of the couch.
The couch is 7.5 feet long and 3 feet wide. The chaise lounge is 6 feet long from back to front. The couch sits 3' high.

MUST PICK UP
Please remember to bring your own blankets to cover and protect the couch.
DO NOT contact me with unsolicited services or offers.

• do NOT contact me with unsolicited services or offers

So, along with two additional (quality) photos, one from a different angle and one extreme close up of the stitching (I mentioned shooting special features up close), this listing gives us a detailed description of the fabric, who the manufacturer was, and:

- It tells us more about the condition
- Where and how it was kept
- Special features/versatility (moving the chaise to either side of the couch)
- Exact dimensions
- Explicitly mentions that it must be picked up
- Thoughtful reminder to bring protection/cover for the couch while transporting

Great copy if you ask me. It's a little hard to read because of the difference in sentence length (short sentences in the first paragraph, long sentences in the second). Keep this in mind. I know it's nit-picky, but we're trying to sell your couch.

The only thing I might add to this is the reason you are selling. Some debate whether this stretches into the "fluff" area, but some folks want to know why it's not good enough for you anymore.

You can simply say something like this: *We're moving and no longer have room for this piece.*

You are moving. Onto your SAILBOAT! Into your TINY HOUSE! (*insert whatever fantastic dream space you have here*)

Now you not only know how to take great photos, but you also know how to write a quality "No-Fat" listing. When that's all filled in, click the CONTINUE button, and let's add a few photos.

Click the *Add / Edit Images* button. Then click *Browse* and find the folder on your desktop where you stored all those pictures you took. We labeled it **To Sell.**

Pick one main image, a second angle, and a closeup if needed.

Once you've uploaded your images, click CONTINUE again. Craigslist will walk you through a series of prompts and security measures, and then prompt you to click on a link if you want to preview your ad.

Once you do this, you can go back and make changes if you don't like the way it looks. If everything looks good, publish the ad.

Now that your ad is live, check your email regularly and make sure you respond promptly to any questions or requests to see the item. Remember, you want to make it as easy as possible for them to give you money.

I want you to be successful, and having this knowledge will ramp up your downsizing. And who couldn't use a few extra bucks to go along with that extra space?

These ad tactics will work across the board. Some of the online selling sites such as Facebook Marketplace are easier, and some might be a little more involved. And while the platform and interface might look different, the quality of your photos and text will be universal. That's what sells your stuff. Don't cut corners.

Okay, that's it for this task! You're getting close now.

ACTION STEP

Using the tips for writing good copy for your listings, list each item from the SELL column in your Room-by-Room Organizer on an online marketplace. Then sit back and wait for random strangers to offer to give you money.

Task 5:
Estate? I Have an Estate?

I'm having a yard sale to sell all the shit I bought at yard sales!

How's your es-state of mind right about now? See what I did there? My jokes are awesome. That's what you want to say, right? I read a book on bad humor. Can you tell?

This entire section is devoted to The Sell. So far in this section, we've talked about different websites where you can list your items. We've gone over some techniques for taking better photos, and I've walked you through the Craigslist process.

But what if you don't want to sell your stuff on *any* website at all. What if:

- You don't have the time to take a bunch of photos
- You don't have the time to upload them
- You don't have the time to post the items and manage the responses
- You have safety concerns about giving your number or email to strangers

I get it. It's a lot of work, and it can be stressful to deal with strangers. So what's your option?

An **Estate Sale**. *Not* a garage sale.

In the overview, I told you to *never have a garage sale. Here's why.*

People who attend garage sales have the perception that your stuff is one small step away from being trash. It's not your fault. It's not your stuff's fault.

It's just what the term GARAGE SALE conjures up.

Usually, garage sales are held outside. The items are lying on the ground or rickety tables. Worse yet, they're in nasty cardboard boxes. People rummage through with pensive expressions, looking for any excuse to haggle over a $0.50 James Patterson novel.

You might have a Gucci bag in your collection, but lay it on the grass and it screams, *"Hey! Bid a dollar! She'll take it – I'm a stone's throw away from being donated!"*

No bueno.

Instead, you are having an *Estate Sale*. (Yes, capitalize it. It makes it fancier.)

Having an Estate Sale is way better than a garage sale because:

- Calling it an Estate Sale elevates the event. Your stuff isn't junk, so don't treat it like junk.
- It's inside, so it's not weather dependent.
- It's great for getting rid of the larger items: sofas and appliances
- **The buyers take it with them when they leave**! This is critical. You don't have to move, deliver, or donate the heavy stuff.

Now, if you don't want to mess with putting on an estate sale yourself, many companies will, for a price, arrange the entire thing. It can be costly but if you don't have the time to mess with listing each individual item, this might be your next option.

They'll charge you in one of two ways:

- **A set percentage:** If they take 35% and the sale generates $10,000, you owe them $3,500. This is the least common method, but it's still used by some companies.

- **Sliding Scale:** Simply put, the more money the sale makes, the lesser the percentage you pay. This is the most common method used. An example might look like this:

Sales:	Percentage Owed:
$5,000- $10,000	50%
$ 10,001 - $15,000	45%
$ 15,001 - $20,000	40%

While going this route will take the burden off of you, it's expensive, and you'll want to do your homework to find a reputable company in your area.

Should you decide to tackle the Estate Sale yourself, the rest of this task will tell you exactly what you need to know.

First, you're going to need one of the tools that you used in Section 2: The **Price Sheet.**
If you recall, there were three columns containing three different prices on that sheet:

What It's Worth
What You Want
What You'll Accept

Next, you'll need to pick a date. Give yourself a couple of weeks to prepare.

- Place an ad in your local paper: DAY, DATE, TIME, ADDRESS & EMAIL

- Make flyers and post them in your local businesses, markets, and coffee shops (include a Google map on your flyer. Send a map link when you respond to emails)
- Post the details on Facebook / Twitter / Instagram and ask your friends to share
- Post on Craigslist to announce the sale
- On your ads, include in big letters: **ITEMS MUST LEAVE WITH YOU ON DAY OF SALE**

Once you've done that, you'll need to enlist the aid of a few friends or family members. These folks are going to be your chaperones on the day of the sale. We'll talk about them later.

Now that you have your date and your chaperones, you need to buy (or make) some labels.

- Feature your "What You Want" price in big READABLE numbers
- Get someone with great handwriting to do this or print them from your computer
- These price tags need to look GOOD. It's all about the impression your creating

Once you have everything labeled, it's time to prepare your home. Think about people you don't know walking through your house. They won't be completely unattended, since you'll have your chaperones there, but you still need to view your home with a critical eye.

If your house has two floors, you'll stage 2 chaperones on the first floor and 2 on the second.

I suggest stopping by your local Home Depot or Lowes and getting some Trimaco paper for your rugs and hardwoods. It's simple brown paper 35" wide and 140' long.

You can get the paper with a sticky backing, but I don't recommend it. I just don't trust that it won't pull up the precious finish from hardwood floors when you go to remove it after the sale.

PRO TIP: As a courtesy, it's always good to inform your neighbors that you'll be having an Estate Sale. Be nice, and your immediate neighbors might let you use their driveway to park the overflow.

THE NIGHT BEFORE THE SALE

Make a few signs that say **DO NOT ENTER** for the doors to rooms that are off-limits to buyers. Your chaperone will curtail any attempts to wander.

Where's your Square?

If you went all in and got yourself a Square device as mentioned earlier in this section, decide where it's going to live on the day of the sale. Whether it's in a coffee mug on the mantel or on top of the refrigerator, make sure everyone on your team knows where to find it.

Then, make sure they also know to **PUT IT BACK** after they've sold an item. This eliminates disorganization. It saves everyone from watching your mom race through your house yelling *"Karen! Where's the blankety-blank square!"*

DAY OF THE SALE

Move extra vehicles (unless you're selling them) to make room for your customers. A buyer might need to access your driveway to load up that couch they just bought, so you don't want to waste time figuring out whose car is blocking it. Take too long and the buyer could change their mind.

PRO TIP: Block your driveway with your car. This prevents people you don't know from parking there. If someone needs to load out an item, move, let them load up, and block it again.

PRO TIP 2: If you're selling one of your vehicles at the estate sale, make sure you have the title and proper paperwork on hand and easily accessible. Don't be digging to find it when you have a customer waiting to give you money.

YOUR SALES TEAM / CHAPERONES

Each of your helpers gets a clipboard or folder with your Price Sheet. It's for **their eyes only**.

Make sure they know not to badger your guests with a heavy sell. They just need to be close and noticeably involved with your sale. A clipboard will identify them as such.

With that price sheet in hand, your helper can now close a deal without having to come find you because they have the important information: What you'll accept.

The tag on the item shows the potential buyer what you want. The Price Sheet tells your helper what you'll accept as your lowest price. If the buyer offers anything in between the two, it's a done deal. Go get the square and close the deal. Or… better yet, take the cash.

And that's where YOU come in. When the cash starts to flow.

- Collect the cash and store it somewhere safe
- On your own copy of the price sheet, note what an item sold for
- Make sure the Square gets back to its special place
- We've all seen Bridezilla. Don't be like that. No stress. No yelling.
- Keep meticulous records. You don't want to have an awkward money moment with family or friends at the end of the day. After all, they're volunteering to help you.

CRITICALLY IMPORTANT: When someone buys an item, it leaves with them. No exceptions.

It will be tempting to take someone's money under the guise of, "We'll come back and get it tomorrow." Don't do this! You will be inviting *their* neurosis into *your* new and uncluttered life.

You've given them an opportunity to get home, look around their own messy house, and say, *"Shit. We don't need that xyz. Call them and tell them we want our money back!"*

If you've done the steps above, you'll likely have a successful estate sale. Yes, there are exceptions, of course. Falling under the heading of *I shouldn't have to say this,* here goes:

- You live in a rural area 30 miles away from anything
- It snowed seventeen inches the night before / rained hellcats and the bridge is gone
- There are six pit-bulls in your yard
- Your barefoot uncle Frank is on the porch, shirtless with a beer. It's 8 am.

You get the drift.

This event could be fun, and it could net you some serious dollars. All the while, clearing out some of the bigger items in one day! That's huge.

So there you have it. Everything you've ever wanted to never know about an Estate Sale. After this, you'll need to pop open a bottle of champagne or your favorite vino and celebrate.

If you're like us, we grabbed a six-pack of High Life and sat in our empty living room with a few white containers of Chinese food.

We were too damn tired to care. Every dollar we raised went into our cruising kitty. By the time we were through, we had close to ten thousand of them. I'll take that.

If you're at that point, scream at the top of your lungs and let yourself be amazed at your BADASSNESS.

By this point, most of your stuff should be gone, but chances are, there were some things that you weren't able to sell. This is normal. Now's the time to build some karma points by donating what's leftover in one fell swoop.

Gather up the non-sellable items, plus any leftover items from your Pretend It's Gone exercise in Section 2. If you haven't already, get rid of everything in the bins you were stashing You've been living without them (or you should have been anyway) and now it's time to say goodbye permanently. See ya!

Call the Salvation Army. Provided your stuff is in *great shape*, they'll send a truck to pick every single bit of it up. That's awesome.

As I've said throughout this course, each person's journey will be different. I've written this book in a way to give every person the flexibility to create their timeline for accomplishing this process along with a detailed road map from point A to point B.

It's all about the options and using what works for you.

There's just one more section left. You've done some serious work.

Hopefully, you're able to see your new life from where you're sitting. Maybe not physically, but in your mind. It just might be the only thing you see because your house is probably empty!

I hope you're getting excited. If not, you will be when I tell you this is the end of this section's tasks!

ACTION STEP

Host an Estate Sale to get rid of a large bulk of your items at once and bring in way more cash than a garage sale. Once your Estate Sale is over, collect any remaining items and donate them, earning you some big-time karma points. Plus, you'll feel amazing.

Section 4:
Going Digital

*"Simplicity is about subtracting the obvious
and adding the meaningful."*
-John Maeda

Congrats on making it to section 4. I'd love to be a fly on
the wall at your house right now.

When Melody and I reached this point in our
downsizing, I remember two distinct emotions that hit
me immediately when my eyes opened every morning.
"Holy shit, what have we done?" followed shortly
thereafter by, *"Holy shit... I can't believe we're about to
pull this off."*

If you're experiencing a bit of uncertainty, I hope it's
accompanied by a great sense of accomplishment and a
lighter consciousness.

Keep moving forward. If it feels like one step forward
and two back, don't focus on that, just keep chipping

away at it. The size of the step is irrelevant. What matters is that you keep moving forward. At the very beginning of this book, I mentioned that you didn't arrive at your overly cluttered life in one week. Don't expect to be free from it in one week. It takes time.

That's why I suggested starting a year before you think you'll need it. If you go through this process two or three times, fine. Most people do. Each time you downsize, you get better at it and more efficient. It also becomes less emotional because you understand the process better.

This section is all about managing your digital footprint. Are you aware of how many digital accounts you have? Subscriptions? A lot of people I've worked with aren't. They signed up, used it for a while, and then got too busy or lost interest but never bothered to cancel because it was "just a pain in the butt to find my password and account info."

Some still paid the monthly fees rather than go through the stress of searching for the information to cancel.

- Kindle Unlimited
- Amazon Prime
- Netflix
- Hulu

You have passwords for Facebook, Gmail, and Instagram, and logins for everything nowadays, from your bank and retirement accounts to your new

Craigslist or Square accounts. It's endless. But we're about to reign it all in.

This section is going to require more brain than brawn. But don't let that trick you into thinking this will be easy or that it can be skipped altogether. Managing your digital clutter is just as important as managing your physical clutter, and imperative if you truly want to enjoy the benefits of your newly uncluttered tiny life.

Some of the things you'll be doing in this section:

- Minimizing your subscriptions (some of which you might forget you even have!)
- Discovering alternative options for storing your photos and documents
- Learning a better way to keep track of your most important passwords
- Discovering a service that allows you to get your mail from anywhere in the world
- Eliminating time-sucking distractions

Now, let's start managing your 1s and 0s.

Task 1:
The 5 Ps

"Proper Preparation Prevents
Piss-poor Performance."
-Charlie Batch

This task is a little different because we're not dealing with physical stuff. Instead, this task is all about getting your records in order. I should warn you, it's a long one.

Having your financial, medical, and personal records organized and easily accessible takes a massive load off of your shoulders when you're cruising. Take it from someone who lost his wallet overboard and had his debit card compromised while in a foreign country... twice.

More seriously, in case of a medical emergency, having important information accessible could mean the difference between life and death.

Download the **Financial Accounts Log** and **Medical Information Form** from the Resource Hub (chrisdicroce.com/tinylife).

FINANCIAL RECORDS

Now it's time to open your **Financial Accounts Log** and fill out each applicable item.

On this list, you'll be recording a lot of *highly sensitive information,* so I don't recommend keeping a physical copy of this around or even just saving it to your laptop.

For maximum security, I recommend you do the following:

1. Fill the Financial Checklist out on your computer and save it to your desktop
2. Email a copy as an attachment to yourself (and your spouse if applicable)
3. Email a copy to a trustworthy family member or friend
4. Delete the copy from your desktop

Doing this removes it from your computer (should it ever be stolen), and by emailing it to yourself, you have a copy that is accessible from anywhere you can access your email. If your computer crashes, you can still access the info on your phone or from another computer.

I wished someone had mentioned this tactic to me earlier. When I lost my wallet, having all of my information in one place would have eliminated a ton of stress. And that's why I'm encouraging you to do this *before* you have an emergency.

This checklist includes:

- Bank accounts
- Retirement accounts
- Credit cards
- Pension information
- Mortgage and personal debt info
- Health savings accounts

Understandably, you may not feel comfortable listing all of this information. The problem with *not* doing this comes when you're sailing abroad and you lose your info or worse yet, someone steals your debit or credit card number, and you have to cancel everything.

Spending an hour or two on the phone with customer service as you try to hunt down old passwords and account numbers gets old rather quickly, not to mention the international roaming fees you're paying if you're abroad like I was.

MEDICAL RECORDS

Along with your financial records, you'll want to consolidate your medical information. I've made that easy for you with the **Medical Information Form**.

I do recommend keeping physical copies of this checklist. You'll want to keep a copy somewhere that is quickly and easily accessible. You should be able to have it in hand in under 30 seconds.

We kept a laminated copy taped to the underside of the lid on our navigation desk. This way we didn't have to dig through any paperwork or search our boat during an emergency. We knew exactly where it was.

I've given you extra space on this checklist to add additional notes and information for your specific needs. The most important items include:

- Blood types for everyone on the boat
- Prescription medications
- Known health conditions
- Eyeglass prescription details
- Allergies to specific medications
- Emergency contact information

MAIL CALL!

If your time home isn't stationary, one thing you'll need to think about is how and where you'll receive mail. These days, there are a ton of ways to go paperless, but there are circumstances where you'll need to receive packages or physical pieces of mail.

Some of you can use a family member or friend's address but when you do that you're relying on other people and putting the burden on them.

If you plan to get a P.O. Box, here's something you should know. If you live on your boat or in an RV, the United States Post Office considers you homeless, and you can't rent a P.O. Box without a home address. I know – kinda obvious to me, too. If I had a permanent mailing address, I wouldn't NEED a P.O. box.

But it's true. When we sold our house and moved aboard, I took a freelance job that landed us in Fort Lauderdale for a year. We decided to get a P.O. box to make things easy. The kind lady at the post office informed us that without a permanent mailing address, the post office considered us homeless and wouldn't let us rent a P.O. box.

And to be honest, having a P.O. box doesn't help you get your mail if you're cruising or traveling full time. You'd again have to rely on someone to check your box and collect your mail for you, again, putting the burden on them.

You can use places like UPS and alternative mailbox services but check their policies and prices carefully. Check to see if they offer forwarding services. If they do, find out what they charge and how the items will be forwarded. (FedEx, U.S. Mail, or UPS).

The service we've been using since 2013 is **St. Brendan's Isle** (sbimailservice.com). They're located in Green Cove Springs, Florida (30 miles NE of St. Augustine) and they've been meeting the needs of traveling doctors and nurses, merchant marines, RVers, and sailors since 1988!

They offer a Cruiser Home Port Package for a reasonable monthly rate. To explain everything they do and how they do it would take some time. I'll break it down quickly for you and then set you loose to find out more if you so choose.

In a nutshell, **their address serves as your legal address**

When you receive new mail, they notify you via email. You can then log into your account and see a scan of the outer envelope. If you want the contents inside to be scanned as a PDF, they can do that for a small additional fee, allowing you to read your mail from anywhere on the planet!

They hold onto your mail and packages until you request them to either be forwarded to you (anywhere in the world) or shredded and disposed of.

A few other features and benefits:

- They're licensed and insured
- Authorized by the Coast Guard to handle boat documentation renewals
- With a bit more paperwork to establish Florida domicile, your mailbox serves as a legal address for your Florida voter registration and driver's license renewals

Check out the cool graphic below illustrating how it all works.

With SBI You Have A Choice

And, if you do decide to sign up for service with St. Brendan's Isle, you can tell them that we referred you (Box 6318) and we'll get a free month of service. So thanks! ;) If you refer others to the service, you get a free month too. Win-win.

ACTION STEP

Download or print the **Financial Accounts Log** and **Medical Information Form** from the Resource Hub (<u>chrisdicroce.com/tinylife</u>) and fill them out. Save them to your computer, then email a copy of each to yourself. Delete the Financial Accounts Log from your computer. If desired, sign up for an account at St. Brendan's Isle for your mail service.

Task 2:
Time for the Big Unsubscribe

"57 channels and nothing's on."
-Bruce Springsteen

Springsteen sang that song in 1992. YouTube wasn't even around then. Now, it has 505,347,842+ channels, and *everything is on.*

These days, we do everything online. We get our news, recipes, movies, videos, fashion advice, and music off the web. Streaming is hotter than ever, and traditional content providers are dying a slow death.

Thing is, it's not just media that has moved into the subscriber platforms. Almost anything you want is available through the mail. Amazon changed the game entirely. And we as consumers swallowed the bait.

Set up an account with your favorite vendor, pay a small monthly fee and you can have beauty products, razors, dog treats, tampons, and already prepared meals at your door.
BAM! No muss. No Fuss.

This is a great thing. It's also a dangerous thing.

In this task, you'll be looking at your mail-order purchases and your digital and box subscriptions with a critical eye. Some of your subscriptions won't even make sense if you're traveling on a boat or in an RV. Tiny house folks may be more stationary, so this might matter a little more to you.

You may have subscriptions that you initially signed up for as a "trial" but then converted to a full paid membership that you forgot to cancel. Or maybe you have a digital subscription that you no longer use, but you forgot you had or, simply don't want to spend the time jumping through their hoops to cancel. They don't make it easy anymore.

You'd be surprised at what you find going through your credit card and bank statements. I recommend looking at your statements from the past 3 months. This will show you repeated charges that you may be able to eliminate.

Let's face it... some subscriptions are incredibly useful. Two examples are:

Amazon Prime: No brainer. We travel full time and have used it all over the world. I'd be lost without my Amazon Prime. The cost is $119 per year ($12.99 per month) at the time of this writing, but it includes free 2-day shipping, free book downloads, and more. Ship one thing per month and it pays for itself very quickly.

Netflix: We use this as well. In fact, Amazon and Netflix are the only two subscription services we kept. Binge-watching whatever Netflix series you're addicted to in the comfort of your cozy space is one of life's simple pleasures. I say this is money well spent.

As I've mentioned throughout the first two sections, you want to keep the stuff you love and use often. If your subscription falls into that category. Keep it.

Here are a couple of examples of subscription services that could go on the chopping block.

Birchbox: High-end beauty products. $10 bucks a month. They just started Birchbox for Men. Can you go back to getting your beauty stuff the old-fashioned way? I think you can.

Bestowed: This company blows my mind. Do you use it? With estimated revenues of over $20 million, somebody is using it. For $25 per month, they send you protein bars and workout videos? Seriously? Please tell me you don't use this. If you do... CANCEL IT! Think of it this way: walking to the store to purchase your protein bar qualifies as "fitness and health." And it's FREE!

Listen, I'm making a joke here, but there are thousands of subscription services that millions of people use. If you're one of them, this is an area you might want to look at. Clutter is clutter, both physical and virtual.

I've said many times in this course, *less doesn't mean nothing*.

We're just trimming some fat and substituting subscriptions that no longer fit in your new life with ones that do. By trimming the fat, we're eliminating emails from your inbox, putting dollars back in your pockets, and freeing up more of your time.

You've worked hard to make better use of your space, do the same with your time. You can buy a new couch or crockpot down the line. You can't buy more time.

That's it for this task!

ACTION STEP

Go through 3 months of bank and credit card statements and look for repeated monthly charges that indicate a subscription of some sort. What can you cancel? What should you keep? Be as discerning as you were with your clothes.

Task 3:
Your Head's Not the Only Thing
in the Clouds

"Hey (hey), you (you) - get off of my cloud."
-The Rolling Stones

I want to get right to it. Throughout this course, you've scrutinized your personal space, examined every object around you with a critical eye. Now we're going to go a bit further and delve into your computer.

Like that junk drawer in the kitchen, your computer can get bogged down, too. And because sometimes hard drives fail, you need to have a backup. We all know this. Call me Professor Obvious. Knowing and addressing are two entirely different things.

My MacBook Pro has suffered not one, but two hard drive crashes in the past few years. Fortunately, I had a backup drive. But there was still a problem: I was working on a job in Atlanta. My external hard drive was on the boat in Fort Lauderdale. What good is your backup if you can't access it?

And this is precisely why I'm going to give you 3 different backup options. You may know about all of them. But are you using any of them?

External Hard Drive: External drives are great. They're cheap, sometimes water and shockproof, and offer as much as 2TB of storage for under a hundred bucks. Great deal and they don't take up any room. I keep ours in a small waterproof pelican case. I suggest buying two and keeping one with you at all times. They're so cheap. Now you can get 1TB flash drives!

Dropbox (dropbox.com): I use Dropbox all the time. It's great for storing your important files and also for sharing files. Dropbox has a free plan with 2GB of storage. Their Plus plan gives you 1TB of storage for just $9.99/mo at the time of this writing. One great thing about the Plus plan is that you get the Mobile Offline Folder feature. This allows you to sync(*) your most important documents to your mobile device so you can access them *without wifi*. If you're on the move at all, the first thing you learn is that wifi is precious and sporadic, so this feature comes in handy.

Google Drive (<u>drive.google.com</u>): The most recognizable name in the world is Google. There's a reason they're the number one cloud storage service on the planet. While Dropbox gives you 2GB for free, Google Drive ups the ante by giving you 15GB. The 1TB plan will set you back about $10 per month (at the moment). Like Dropbox, it can automatically sync with your mobile devices and computers.*

(*)NOTE: If you use Dropbox or Google for syncing your files, you'll want to turn off the automatic syncing feature if you're using a hotspot or paid data service. Otherwise, you'll eat up your data very quickly, and may see a bill from your data provider for hundreds of dollars. Don't ask me how I know this.

The huge benefit of storing in the cloud becomes obvious if your computer crashes or if you just need access to something quickly. The cloud allows you to download a backup of important documents via wifi from *wherever you are*. No need to hunt down your external drive and wait for it to boot up.

You can take the belt and suspenders approach (as I do) and use both. An external drive for your entire computer system backup and then one of the free cloud options for work documents, important medical or financial records, or just photos and music. I use all 3!

The sky's the limit. I'm sorry... it was just too easy to drop that one.

Now that you have 3 great storage options, I suggest you consider using them for:

- Your Medical and Financial checklists (and other important documents)
- Photos: If you have photos you want to keep, scan them and store them digitally
- Music: Import your music from the physical CD to the digital world and get rid of the CD

Better to do this while you have high-speed wifi. It may take a while for your files to sync, so set it to sync while you finish some last-minute tasks around the home.

Like going back through that box of stuff you're saving "just in case." You might find that your mindset has changed over the last few sections, so there may be some things you can more easily part with now.

ACTION STEP

Choose your backup storage option/s and back up your files! Don't wait to back them up. Do it now. Remember what I said in the first task in this section about proper preparation.

Task 4
What's the Password?

*"I changed my password to 'fortnight'.
Apparently, that was two week."*
-Unknown

You know, I can remember a time when I used to know my friends' phone numbers. At this very moment, I still remember the first phone number I ever had CL9-8358. But I can't seem to remember my Apple login username and password.

In the not-too-distant past, whenever I signed up for a new account, I'd put the login information and password in the 'Notes' section of my phone. It was haphazard at best. Disorganized and stressful at its worst.

How many passwords do you have? When I was putting together this book, I counted mine. I have 15! My wife has 10x that. Many of you are the same. And that's what I'll be talking about in this task: Password Managing Apps.

Today's technology is awesome. Without it, my wife and I probably wouldn't have been able to realize our dream of living and working remotely.

Since we moved aboard in 2012, in addition to the entire Gulf of Mexico and Eastern Seaboard of the United States, we've sailed to Cuba, Mexico, Belize, and Guatemala.

Living life as a digital nomad requires us to have different accounts for lots of things, and for security purposes, we have secure passwords and use a different one for each account. I am an admitted scatterbrain. I need some sort of organizer for, if nothing else, my passwords.

If you have too many passwords in too many different places, it's time to gather them all up and put them in one easily accessed spot where all you have to remember is ONE password.

Almost all of the good ones require a monthly subscription. I know... I just told you to get rid of your monthly subscriptions! Not in this case. Sometimes an exception needs to be made.

Here are 4 Password Managers out there to help you get organized.

1Password (1password.com): 1Password has been around for a while and it runs on macOS, Windows, and Android platforms. Once you create your password 'vault', 1Password allows you to sync it with your Dropbox or iCloud so you can access your vault offline. If you prefer not to sync your passwords, you can access your vault over wifi. The other great thing 1Password lets you do is to share your vaults with family members.

Using the 1Password app, you can create 'teams' and family accounts that allow you to selectively share vaults, and even control who can make changes to those passwords.

There is a free version, but it's limited. Their subscription plan requires a monthly subscription.

Dashlane (dashlane.com) Much like 1Password, Dashlane allows you to sync across multiple devices with their paid plan. Unlike the former, it's only available for Mac and Windows. They do offer a free account that allows access to your passwords through a single device of your choice.

What makes it different than 1Password is that no matter what option you choose, Dashlane does not store a copy of your master password in any form. It remains only with you. If you lose it, they have no way of recovery. As they say, not even a hacker (or government agency) could access your passwords without knowing your master password.

Premium accounts let you synchronize your passwords across multiple devices, perform account backups, share more than five items, give you access to the web app, and entitle you to Dashlane's customer support.

LastPass (lastpass.com) This is my personal favorite. Over 25 million people use this service. They have a free version, a premium version, and a family option that allows you 6 different premium licenses to share. It offers all the bells and whistles like autofill when you shop online with one of the accounts you have listed in LastPass. It's a super cool app at a great price. I use it on all my devices.

KeePass (keepass.info) This is a FREE open-source program for macOS and Android. It's not fancy but it does exactly what you need. Keeps all your passwords secure and in one place.

So there you go. Do a Google search for "Password Managers" and you'll find more options than you'll know what to do with. I could have given you a top 10, but why? I'm here to make things easier, not overload you with options.

Getting close now!

ACTION STEP

Choose a Password Manager to help you manage your passwords. This keeps you from forgetting them, and it's also more secure than writing them down somewhere.

Task 5:
Distraction Faction

Stop getting distracted by things that have nothing to do with your goals!

Easier said than done!

We are just about through. It's been so cool getting to accompany you on this journey. I take great pride in nudging you towards your tiny life goals. It's hard to believe we're one task away from the end of the book.

That said, I won't go off on a tangent and get all touchy-feely on you. That would be going off-topic, which is exactly the subject of this task: Distractions.

THE DIVIDED MIND AND THE MYTH OF MULTI-TASKING

You've probably heard by now that multitasking is a myth. The brain cannot focus on more than one thing at a time. Like reading a text and driving, or typing an email and listening to your spouse or partner. In the rapid attention-switching, things get missed. And it's killing us.

- 25% of all traffic fatalities are caused by distracted drivers
- 58% of all teen fatalities are related to distracted driving

When they're not killing us, they're robbing us of valuable time and interaction. Standing in line at the grocery store or bank, every single person stares at their phones. Take a look around the airport next time you're waiting to board a flight. We've lost the ability to exist without constant stimulation. We've lost the ability to be entertained by the moment in which we exist.

What in the hell does any of this have to do with downsizing?

Nothing. Until you put it into context and consider the time you spend checking your Facebook and other social media profiles. How many games do you play when you should be focused on something else?

I read a statistic recently (which caused me to put this task here) that stated:

Employees ages 18 to 34 rack up 70 minutes a day on mobile device distractions and 48 minutes on personal tasks unrelated to the job they're being paid to perform.

That's almost two hours every day. And that's just during work hours. How many minutes are wasted in an entire 24 hours?

Thinking – and then rethinking about the way you spend your time is completely related and connected to living a simpler life. You here because you're attempting to climb out from under a mountain of clutter. And the clutter isn't just clothes, dishes, tools, and paperwork.

Clutter infiltrates our lives in so many ways.

- 24-hour news channels
- 24-hour drive-thru restaurants
- On-demand everything

We're overstimulated and undernourished. Overpromised and underdelivered. Overworked and underappreciated.

For this task, I want you to take note of the time you spend answering texts, browsing Facebook, and playing games on your phone or laptop. I simply want you to notice it. Write it down the way you would if you were keeping track of a diet. Do it for one day. If you find that you waste minimal time on these endeavors, great. March on.

If, however, you find that the shit you need to get done isn't getting done because you keep distracting yourself, then I challenge you to delete these distractions from your phone and actively change your focus. Life is flying by. Time is a finite resource. And the only place where success comes before work is in the dictionary.

That's it! I end almost every section with the hope that you've gotten inspired and encouraged to go after your new tiny life. The hope that you've been able to visualize, energize, and actualize your path. To a simpler, less cluttered, and happier life.

Congratulations.

ACTION STEP

Do an audit of how your spending (or wasting) your time. How can you downsize your distractions so that you can become a more productive, happier, fulfilled version of yourself?

Conclusion: Happy Hour

Live the life you've imagined.

For 11 years, I had that quote pasted to the front of my refrigerator. I read it every morning when I grabbed the almond milk for my coffee. I drank that coffee in my 2000 Ford Ranger pickup truck driving to a job I hated.

On my office door I had another quote, a poem written by Emily Dickinson, *Dwell in Possibility.*

The poem is so simple. I find it beautiful because to me, it speaks to those who feel as if they live their lives in a never-ending loop. Which I was doing back then. I was not living the life I imagined, nor was I dwelling in possibility. I was in the loop. Wake Up - Go to Work - Pay the Bills - Repeat.

How I let myself get to that point is a long and winding road. And, it's irrelevant. What's relevant is that I recognized it and decided that I needed to change it.

The day I decided to put my house up for sale was terrifying. Second only to the day that I walked into my boss's office to give my notice that I was leaving. When I told the president of my company that I was quitting to move onto my sailboat, do you know what he did? He stood up and hugged me. A bear hug that nearly cracked my ribs.

Then he said, "Man, I wish I did that when I was younger. Good for you. Go knock the shit out of it. Whatever *it* is."

I assume that you bought this book because of your desire, your goal to downsize your life. I'm confident that if you were successful in each one of these tasks, that goal is closer to you now than ever before. Now is not the time to quit. Stay focused. Keep your eye on the prize.

For life is indeed short. For decades we've been fed the lie that money is our greatest asset. It's not. Time is our greatest asset. Spend it wisely.

Now – go out there and knock the shit out of it. Whatever *it* is.

All the best my friend. I wish you love and much joy in your new uncluttered life. If we meet on the water or out on the road, the beers are on me!

Take care,
Chris

P.S. If you've gotten anything positive from this book, I would love if you could leave a review. Your review can help others who may be looking to downsize find this book. Reviews also help me immensely as an independent author. Thank you.

You can find more about me and my other books at chrisdicroce.com.

Other Books by Chris DiCroce

The Quiet Goings On

The Quiet Goings On is a collection of original short stories and poems about life, grown from the dirt of hardship and pain with slivers of triumph and humor...for those who don't mind a little digging.

Whether it's an unexpected rescue in the Mexican desert, the son who comes to terms with his irreverent father, or the massage therapist who has to reconcile with herself, one thing remains constant – DiCroce's characters simply refuse to give up.

Instead, they experience transformative epiphanies both great and small; existing within the restraints of loneliness, acceptance, guilt, contemplation, and hope.

Burning Man

One week ago, Nashville music legend Dash Nelson was on the way down. His music, iconic. Revered. He's got one more record in him and it just might be his best one yet. On the morning after the record release party for Heavy Clutch, Dash is roused from a scotch-induced slumber with the news that his long-time manager and best friend, Paul West, was found dead.

Dash abandons his family, friends, and his record to keep a promise he made to Westie many years ago. A promise that he's certain will land him in prison. When Westie's body goes missing from the morgue, rumors circulate. A mysterious offshore transfer brings the FBI to Nashville, but Dash is nowhere to be found.

After a cross-country road trip and a sacred burial ceremony that pushes Dash to the limits of his own sanity, he ends up in a tiny Western Caribbean island to fulfill one final wish for Westie. An unexpected turn of events leaves him fighting for his life aboard a sailboat with Westie's biggest secret.

From Dash and Westie's aeonic friendship comes BURNING MAN, a simmering novel that twists in the grasp of DiCroce's unique storytelling. If you're a fan of

Carl Hiaasen, Tom Robbins, or Tom McGuane, you're certain to love this novel.

You Gotta Go To Know

"Every minute you spend wishing you did something is a minute you spend not doing it."

If you've ever wanted to sell it all, buy a boat, and sail away, this is a book you'll want to read. Join Chris and Mel on their journey through the decisions, challenges, and triumphs of embracing a minimalist lifestyle to move onto a sailboat full-time.

Tired of the status quo and needing a change, Chris and Melody (along with their dog Jet) quit their jobs and sold their Nashville home and nearly everything they owned to buy a 35-foot sailboat, live aboard, and cruise into the sunset in search of adventure.

Once on board, they discovered that their greatest triumphs often came from their greatest challenges. Champagne wishes and caviar dreams soon fell prey to their bologna sandwich and Miller High Life budget. Boat breakdowns, tropical storms, and over-extended bank accounts brought them face to face with the reality that things don't always go as planned. But sometimes... that's the best plan.

This is the story of a leap of faith -- from making the decision, finding the right boat, downsizing, and finally telling friends, family, and bosses. Light-hearted, humorous, and occasionally sad, this short memoir will draw you in you with its unique look at life on a sailboat and the emotions that come with it. Chris and Melody's story will inspire you to go after your dreams and follow a path less traveled, whether it be on a sailboat, a van, RV, or any other vehicle for travel and adventure.

What's Up Ditch!

If you're thinking about doing a boat trip down the Atlantic Intracoastal Waterway, whether by sailboat, powerboat, or trawler, this is a book to add to your arsenal of information.

What's Up Ditch! is a personal perspective and guide based on observations and the navigation logs of Chris DiCroce, an avid sailor who has traveled the ICW on his sailboat more than six times. He discusses how much boat you really need, how to figure out fuel usage, VHF radio protocol, tides, currents, and more. He also walks you through situations you'll encounter along the waterway, from hailing a bridge to maximizing your budget over the course of this 1000 + mile trip.

What's Up Ditch! is not your typical "waterway guide." It's not a roadmap or anchorage guide. Instead, it gives you the practical knowledge that other guides don't talk about.

The ICW is "back-alley America at six miles an hour" and can take sixteen days or sixteen weeks. It's a trip full of challenges and learning opportunities, and this book addresses a lot of what you'll need to know. From the Dismal Swamp to the Virginia Cut, the Georgia mudflats to Florida, you'll get a viewpoint you may not have read in the past. The Atlantic ICW will test your navigation skills, boat-handling skills, and your patience, but in the end, it will reward you with stunning scenery and an experience you'll not soon forget.

If you've ever thought about doing the ICW, or even if you've done some or all of it, there's something here for you. It's a no-nonsense approach with Chris' usual bad jokes and some well-placed sarcasm. Beware, you magenta line hugging boaters... there's something in there about you as well!

What's Up Ditch! will challenge you and encourage you. It will break down and dissect some of the issues that might be keeping you from doing one of the coolest trips we have right here in America.

About the Author

Chris DiCroce is an author, a songwriter, and -- a quitter.

In 2012, he quit the rat-race, sold his Nashville home and nearly everything he owned to move aboard a small sailboat, in search of a simpler life. Since that time, he's authored several Amazon bestselling books, written for TV shows, and sailed to eight countries.

A staunch minimalist, DiCroce quietly champions the virtues of a simpler life through podcast interviews and speaking engagements. His pieces on travel and minimalism have been featured in major magazines, and he's been featured on popular podcasts including *Speaking of Travel*, *Boat Radio International*, and the *Tiny House Lifestyle Podcast*.

He's currently working on his next novel from his favorite taqueria in Baja, Mexico where he lives part-time with his wife Melody.

To find out more and sign up for his newsletter, visit chrisdicroce.com.